Hidden

Hidden

Reflections on Gay Life, AIDS, and Spiritual Desire

Richard Giannone

Fordham University Press | New York 2012

Library of Congress Cataloging-in-Publication Data

Giannone, Richard.
    Hidden : reflections on gay life, AIDS, and spiritual desire / Richard Giannone.—1st ed.
       p.   cm.
    ISBN 978-0-8232-4184-2 (cloth : alk. paper)
    1. Giannone, Richard.   2. Catholic gay men—New York—New York—Biography. 3. Care of the sick.   4. Caring—Religious aspects—Catholic Church.   I. Title.
BX4705.G525A3   2012
282.092—dc23
[B]

                                                                  2011047353

Printed in the United States of America
14 13 12   5 4 3 2 1
First edition

In memory of
Nellie Cordileone Giannone and Marie Rose Giannone
and for Frank

Contents

But our true Mother Jesus, he alone bears us for joy and for endless life. . . .

—Julian of Norwich, *Showings*

1

An Unfurnished Life

Truly, you are a God who hides himself.

—Isaiah 45:15

Chance has determined the most important things of my life. The coming of a stranger was a telling instance of a rewarding accident that I couldn't have imagined. His appearance held an advantage to be snatched from lucky chances. His guy-next-door good looks, his affecting personal story, his simplicity, his gentle disposition and spiritual desire—it was all entirely improbable. Improbable, also, that I would entrust my heart's secrets and place my future plans in him.

He came in 1981, just in the nick of time. I was forty-seven. I'll save your doing the math; I am now closing in on seventy-five, appreciatively beyond the threescore and ten allotted in the Psalms. His arrival began a friendship that was the great blessing of my life. And I am haunted by the fear that I will forget how cut off I was before this man broke into my buffered existence. Remembering such a favor helps protect me from the hits of aging that could entrap me anew.

Back then I stayed home most of the time at my desk, reading, correcting student essays, or hunching over a Smith-Corona electric typewriter, pecking away without concentration. Stacks of books, many unread, awaited sorting. A few pieces of thrift-shop furniture scattered on a threadbare cranberry-red tribal rug from Lake Van in eastern Turkey equipped the place, a container for thought. A friend once commented that my three rooms seemed to be waiting for someone to occupy them. At the very least, my spirit needed refurbishing.

In the 1970s and '80s being gay didn't evoke, as it presently does, a shrug of the shoulders. Gay life in those decades was menaced by shame and therefore essentially concealed. Even some of those who were not openly homophobic held homosexuals in wary disdain.

Anxiety about getting sick and dying had locked me into fearful self-concern that verged on emotional shutdown. Life as I knew it and hoped it would be was dying out as a fusillade of deadly organisms stealthily attacked gay men. Swollen lymph nodes, signs of infections, popped up during routine physical examinations. In the spring of 1981 five young men in Los Angeles came down with pneumonia from the cytomegalovirus, the herpes virus that usually resolves on its own but was life-threatening in these men. Parasitic pneumonias associated with Third World countries and rare skin tumors ordinarily found in elderly Mediterranean men were appearing in clusters of healthy young gay men in San Francisco and New York. The final quarter of the twentieth century unleashed strange agents of physical dread.

Extinction shrouded gay life. Death wore a public face. Like police raiding a gay bar, the disease outed even the most closeted gay men with a stigmatizing sweep. Private lives became public issues. A cold twilight had settled on my life and the people around me. I might say, with only slight risk of overstatement, that I was growing unaccustomed to being with people. To live happy, goes a French saying, live hidden. Well, I settled just to live.

With all its resources and expertise, medical science remained clueless about the cause of these malignancies until 1983, when Luc Montagnier at the Pasteur Institute in Paris identified a suspect virus. Later that year Anthony Gallo at the National Cancer Institute in Washington cultivated the virus for further investigation and human testing. The cause of these opportunistic diseases of the old and undeveloped places, now atypically presented in urban young men, was found and dubbed AIDS. The name has always struck me as a speciously friendly acronym for so mortal an enemy. *Plague, scourge, pestilence,* and *contagion* work better. It was a gnarly pathogen that kept developing new strains. Research offered a dim hope for treatment and cure.

Epidemic disease of high mortality is not specific to a certain time or place. Neither is sexual desire mixed with distress a new form of torment. HIV/AIDS is current history and an old story at the same time. My experience similarly combines recent events with past disturbances.

As AIDS spread, the disease became an emblem of rampant evil. Laws across the country singled out people with the affliction. The knowing transmission of HIV was a crime in many states. Failure to disclose one's medical status to a partner meant prosecution. Cuba had detention camps for people suffering from the disease. Stigma was criminalized. To emphasize the public slaying endured by sufferers, some political crusaders replaced the neutral clinical language of "dying from AIDS" with the nuclear "killed by AIDS." It was a massacre. Hate reigned. Though little about the syndrome was understood, much was felt and suffered at the very vortex of human desire and need. Sexual intimacy was a minefield of damaging effects yet to be born. Fear charged even the little things of mundane life. Contact with body fluids was like touching a plutonium trigger.

Psychological depth charges exploded firmly implanted anxieties in me. Low-lying dreads went beyond sexual hookups with other men to my essential human identity. My personal experience in the New York gay subculture gave me good reason to be vigilant about safety. Sex in the city during the volcanic late 1960s and 1970s, for all the nostalgic celebrations, was not an HBO series of spiffy adventures. It was combat against unseen adversaries that in retrospect presaged the AIDS crisis. A year and a half after I arrived in August 1967 at thirty-two raring to make up for missed experiences in the Midwest, the pagan in me pitched a tent in the freewheeling sensual fray.

One of the lurking enemies at the time was hepatitis B, and I contracted it. The infection almost killed me. I went to the hospital when snow was on the ground in early March 1969 and left as the sun warmed the early June air. My mother and sister celebrated Mother's Day by visiting me in the hospital. They brought pink carnations, which to them marked the love of living mothers (white flowers honored death mothers). After they asked how I was, Giannone female love moved under full steam. They opened the Venetian blinds of my hospital room to let in the sunlight. They covered their apprehension by bustling about smoothing the bed sheets and asking overcontrolling questions about the food. I wanted to say something funny.

While hospitalized, I fell into a hepatic coma for nearly a week. Confinement to bed and the hospital's pathogenic air led to bacterial pneumonia. The city life I wanted so much to be a part of passed me by that season. A damaged liver takes time to regenerate. Several more months went into gaining back weight and strength. The return of self-respect was another matter. Recovering from liver disease set in as a way of living and of looking at myself. Forty-some years later, I have yet to enjoy a glass of wine.

After I recuperated from a near-death experience, remorse was strong, but so too was the pull of having a meaningful gay life. Sexual desire in my mind competed with survival. My imagination of disaster projected a medical record solely of infectious diseases. Enough was enough. Sex became synonymous with destruction of the gift of health. Sometimes illness is also a metaphor. Contact with the mortal side of sexual disease exposed me to the assaults from the serpents of self-loathing. I had to love myself enough to protect myself. But how? How can a gay man be a good steward of this gift of his body when his sexuality bears the burden of recrimination and religious censure? Doesn't love require a certain abandon? It's hard to imagine safe love.

No longer one to live precariously, I gave up sex and took refuge in concealment. That was in the mid-1970s, before we knew about HIV, but gay men felt the impact of its rampant precursors, hepatitis B and various strains of amoebas creating intestinal ulcerations that made it easier for HIV to infect people. With a wounded dolphin's instinct for danger, I sensed risks in the first inexplicable symptoms and headed for shelter. Trepidation hemmed me in, but fear, mind you, taught me lessons that complacency would not have. I planned to hide out until the swirl of furtive diseases faded away. That indefinite day of reprieve never arrived. Instead, the 1960s era of sexual exploration and freedom vanished. The swarm of HIV/AIDS agents began to overrun gay life, and the city blew up in our faces.

The age of restriction and captivity set in. Gay men were seizing up with loneliness or hard drugs, or by having sex. Sexual desire excited and annihilated. It was not a matter of looking for love in the wrong places; rather, as Tristan and Isolde grieve in five spellbound hours, love was death. One measureless modern catastrophe was wiping out all youth and accolades, and almost the era itself.

By 1981, as the HIV/AIDS epidemic spread unabated, I was living in deep cover two blocks from the meatpacking district of the far west corner of Greenwich Village. At that time, the area was obscure and unmanicured with a drug vibe, by no means sought after and therefore less expensive than other parts of New York. The stench of rotting animal parts caught between cobblestones hung in the air. Rundown market buildings with loading docks defined an industrial Manhattan of manual labor scarcely evident anymore. The shabby milieu with edge-of-the-city feel suited my calculated withdrawal.

Everyone tried to find a way of managing or forgetting sadness. Those who could not forget were the ones infected. My strategy was, I see in retrospect, less to dodge the bullet than to handle my fear of life fraught with human relations. Habit provided a numbing ease. Leaving home meant moving on automatic pilot. I took the A train to Columbus Circle for the D train to the Bronx to give my classes at Fordham University, hold office hours, and attend department meetings.

The classroom was a safe harbor. Young, morally fresh, and at that time removed from the HIV tornado, my Fordham students got me out of myself. Their investment in literature sustained mine. Whether discussing Dante or Faulkner, we were reminded that the hurt and wonder around us partook of the hurt and wonder of all time. The journey of a medieval pilgrim through other worlds coursed into the slogging of a proud, hapless, and dysfunctional Mississippi family bearing one of their own forty miles to burial in Jefferson. What the Florentine says in the *Paradiso* explains how poetry and fiction helped us lead our lives through modern dark places on Christopher Street and beyond.

> Here we contemplate the art which so much love adorns, and we discern the good by reason of which the world below becomes the the world above.

Outside a teaching routine I was fretfully lost. I did go to the opera, but it was like going to Mars for otherworldly entertainment while the curtain was coming down on the spectral planet Earth. Lifeless souls with heedless eyes roamed the once-jaunty Village.

By 1981, I was losing my battle against negativity. I strained to forsake the basic needs of my body, the site of peril. Secretly I wished that I could dispose of my body to escape its vulnerability and death. Fear, I feared, could permanently take me away from people, and from God. I was alive and too worried to see survival as testimony of his kindness and call to responsibility. Having been protected so far, I didn't know what to do with being spared. Sex was out of bounds and on the way to extinction, taking the possibility of human fulfillment with it. Fighting hormones is warfare to the end. A Jesuit friend warned me that sexual abstinence was an objectionable task. It was. I never got used to it. Abstention from sexual relations could be harmful to one's health. It was wringing my soul dry.

The brunt of malaise hit me in late afternoon, as it always has. Looking for repose wherever I could find it, I frequently walked twelve blocks from my apartment on Jane Street to St. Joseph's Church on Sixth Avenue and Washington Place for the weekday 5:30 evening Mass. I didn't know where else to go. Physical movement got me out of myself. Taking my time going from home through triangular Abingdon Square Park, one of New York's oldest and most intimately peaceful green spaces, down Bleecker Street, and across bustling Sheridan Square and Washington Place to church prepared me to pay attention to the unhurried, unvarnished words of scripture. The accounts of spiritual search in the Hebrew and Greek texts breathed life into my ennui.

Love of God did not send me to the liturgy. As an adult, I was not religious. Catholicism with its respect for an inner life evolving while my body and mind were developing did speak to me as a youngster. Jesus's message that I was part of a life beyond my own corresponded with my feeling of not being whole. We, even kids, were more than the sum total of parts and data. Regrettably, early religious instruction neglected to show that this man Jesus worked and suffered in soot and smells among oppressed people. Jesus seemed a laminated card. Grace came not from his life but the church as institution, which tended to misinterpret and misconstrue itself for God.

The Catholic Mass, however, addressed my young hunger for ceremony. I was delighted that the liturgy was about a simple meal offering infinite satisfaction. But trappings obscured the food at the table. Legal formality imposed from the top down to be passively received concealed the gifts. Dutiful fodder did not satisfy the hunger I had for a meaningful life, for God. God, as the Decalogue commanded, was always before me, but God was remote and abstracted from flesh. The divine was as skillfully evasive as Godot in Samuel Beckett's play.

I wanted God to be as alive and next to me as the wracked bodies of people with AIDS. I had long ago rejected the image of God fostered in high school as an Irish cop in favor of a blurred, tattered servant, in fact, one with a woman's soul embodying motherly concern and self-giving, yet free of the maternalism that mimics patriarchal excesses. What remained for me after dismissing church legalism was the Mass. The liturgy was Christianity, that and nothing more. And that was sufficient. After all, the Eucharist was a love feast and thanksgiving centered on the human body. What else need the rite contain?

Finding my share in this pledge of God's grace was and remains the hard part. The church scorns homosexuality. The church offers no access to basic human needs of gay men and lesbians for a prayerful inner life. Our relations go unblessed. Magisterial condemnation has led to subordination and alienation from the fullness of life. But the sacred rite of love is still there—for all. The table has a place for what is in the gay heart and mind. One has to reclaim that place. The route back to the table lies in knowing that doctrine and judgment are not belief.

My reclamation originates before Vatican Council II (1962–65) in an immigrant Catholicism that stressed obedience and held no brief for doubters and those of us with little faith and many questions. A patriarchal authoritarian church served the useful purpose of assimilating the foreign-born but fell short of helping their more educated children. A Sunday school theology prevailed with naïve theism instilled by rote.

One learned simplistic orthodoxies to prop up superstitious venerations that distracted from service to gospel. Bringing historical or literary judgments to scripture and church tradition that mark a mature faith was kept in check. The church actually forbade reading the Bible.

Prohibition was of a piece with dominance. The hierarchy asserted a sexist authority by enforcing inflexible spiritual identities, as though the spirit, divine or human, could be regulated. The clergy was up to its old manner of a stern father dealing with benighted children. The church tried to control souls to save them, and it failed in both purposes. What its too-rigid conception of God succeeded in achieving was emptying belief of the struggle that I experienced and, I now see, as constituting authentic faith.

Dogmatism went deeper to drain the sacraments of the presence of the divine that scripture said dwelled in all creation. God, we were taught, was in our midst, except for the love between two women and that between two men. Same-sex bonds were consigned outside of grace. Grace, of course, was defined and meted out by self-styled celibate bishops. But there was always, I sensed, the true grace of Jesus's sacrifice.

In the end, for the end, I did believe that an eradicable vitality pulsed in the world, even though the power that might free me to be part of the fullness of life escaped me. I did not feel truly alive. I felt that something was lacking in me. To this day, I feel incomplete. Something has always been missing. And something was short-circuiting my emotional life. I felt fear and experienced raw anxiety. When it came to receiving praise or the affection of others, I was blocked. Buffered feelings rendered me too weak to be loved.

As a boy I thought that I would grow out of this restriction just as I would cast off knickers for breeches. While learning the Baltimore catechism in grammar school, I couldn't wait to be an adult with authority over my soul so that I could know God shorn of institutional representations. I was searching, as long I could remember, for a way to live in a world of freedom that was thwarted by religion.

Jesus had several messages, some overlooked, some misread; Jesus said nothing about sex. The church, ever ready to go after pleasure while ignoring Jesus's tolerance and its own guilt, picked up on our obstinate modern preoccupation with sex and sexuality. Ecclesiastical authority amplified society's message that a gay person had no birthright to an inclusive life of love by calling such love a sin. The prohibition effectively reduced the very word *God* to a moral and political weapon to put homosexuals down and exclude them. A deep, black, inexpressible conviction whispered that my inborn nature required pardon and a cure.

How one thinks of oneself affects her or his relationship with God. Homosexuality was a sin, a crime, and an illness. By these verdicts, God could have nothing to do with gay kids. Menaced on all sides, one did not know where to place trust. All I asked for, as a young person, was that the forces of law and order not catch me. But as the culture grew more tolerant, I saw that even when my body was not imperiled, my soul was by early condemnation.

The lesson of alienation comes easily to a malleable young consciousness and stays. The cumulative effect is toxic. The pain is insupportable. No child, or adult for that matter, could hold the feeling of not counting in her or his heart. The cross tells the Christian that innocent suffering has significance, at the same time that the church inflicts pain. Historically, a cultural aspect of Christian love rests on glib hatred of others—sometimes Jews, reformers, nonconformists, and gays. This hard side of Christianity distanced me from the church. Professed "religious" Christians were the last people to whom I would bring a burden of shame or a need for understanding. People without faith seemed more tolerant and Christian. As for censorious believers, well, after more than seventy years, I still cannot fathom the behavior that habitually disgraces others at the center of their identity.

I am simplifying complex matters here. The impediments to faith undeniably go further back in time and run far deeper than sexuality and my personal quarrel with the church. Faith, doubt, and nonbelief take shape from the cultural surroundings that mediate spiritual responses to immaterial forces. Nihilism surrounds modern life. The air we breathe flows with hostile agents that shield us from religion, at least from trusting current religious forms and bodies. As the secular mind has swapped history for social studies, it concurrently has traded ultimate concerns for power politics. The unseen and mysterious have disappeared. The outcome is tangible. Once a pervasive influence in the public sphere and amenable to faith, religion in our time seems irrelevant to interior search, for some even opposed to open inquiry and personal transcendence. And yet spiritual desire is very much with us as yearning sways indecisively through religious institutions unmoored from the way people live.

Not to be discouraged, a part of me, a better angel, was always saying *yes* to that source of life that led to Jesus's self-donation despite the church's *no* to my sexuality. The human spirit has its own way of resisting containment. My way was to stay the course to St. Joseph's Church in my Greenwich Village neighborhood. The fifteen-minute walk, more or less meditative, granted a soothing rhythm that anchored the day in a clean, well-lighted, sacred space. Unlike the impersonal mammoth of Catholicism, St. Joseph's was tiny, local, and living at the mercy of felt experience. Here I sensed an entity, not an organization, that conveyed the original meaning of *church* as "belonging to the Lord."

The parish community was founded in 1829. The church is a fine architectural place that expresses more than Catholicism's self-conscious monument to its own authority. Made of white granite, the church has a vernacular combination of Federal and Greek revival styles inflected with two Doric columns. The physical structure dates back to 1833, which makes it the oldest Catholic building in New York. Its social history also drew me. Dorothy Day, one of the founders of the Catholic Worker movement who committed her life to feeding and housing the homeless while working through nonviolence for social justice, attended Mass at St. Joseph's. Hans Küng, the eminent Swiss theologian who challenged papal infallibility, one Sunday evening spoke there on religious liberty. These reformers and other dissidents, who struggled to live the radical gospel call, interlaced the building's traditional stained-glass windows and old cement with progressive ideals.

St. Joseph's also serves nearby New York University and other schools. That gives the setting a certain familiarity. Officially, the title is the University Parish of Saint Joseph. The contemporary mood of the varied parishioners in the oldest Catholic house of worship in New York opened its grand, dark red doors to me as a guest making gestural visits. If a precarious haven, the church was in spite of everything a hideout from God and the plague. With my visceral aversion to attention, I sat in a rear pew where I was like one of those nonconversant lay brothers at a charterhouse, who remained silent in their own oratory while the divine office was chanted and bowed at the appropriate places. Hearing the congregants at St. Joseph's without vocally joining in was my way of learning and bearing passive witness.

Being acted upon felt right. I was a stone over which the flow of words washed to smooth the coarse surface of my rough mood. Day after day, month after month, the cycle of saints' days and feasts meant little to me. I enjoyed no change in season. Holidays turned into mourning, and all the songs flattened into laments. Jesus's daily life and messages alone drew me. Even though I could not live up to his instructions of self-giving, I accepted as morally valuable his directives to take up a life of self-abnegation in service to the poor, sick, and downtrodden.

I believed in Jesus's teaching, but I could not grasp how he incarnated the divine nature. He came into the world and left it as we do. Could Jesus be a mortal human and still be all that he says he is? If he is like us in all things except sin, then Jesus is not like us. Holy scriptures, with details that get in the way, satisfied my soul. *Peace, love, faith,* and *heartfelt compassion* seeped up from the ancient past as whispering words requiring flesh-and-bone to give them new life that builds us up. The liturgy suggested a locus of meaning beyond dogma or political mandate to a vital self-esteem, to a way one could live and act without a defensive ego.

The Lord's Supper offered a way of partaking of divine purposes. But how does the message formulated in the arid steppes and coastal strip of ancient Palestine under Roman tyranny play out in the grim and contagious blood of the AIDS devastation around 14th Street? The teaching of Jesus had to have fruit among us or it was a lie. For all its incomprehensibility, the notion of healing by and union with something everlasting became identified in my mind with forces that can never be defeated, even by almighty AIDS. My frailty counted on such power. Vocally and silently brought to the altar by the handful of us at the 5:30 liturgy, this irrational trust underlay the spirituality of disease circulating inaudibly in the clamorous politics of the AIDS disaster.

And so I went to St. Joseph's. Worship was private; it was not for me the communal experience Jesus meant it to be. Community is the heart of Christianity. Like communication, community all too frequently fails. Because I stood in tension, mostly in conflict, with the collective conduct of the church, I rarely went to the liturgy on the Lord's Day, when large assemblies gathered. The decision was quirky but felt just. Again, because every day brought the duty to struggle with doubt and personal sinfulness, I paid no special attention to officially designated "holy days of obligation." Worship was only about Jesus's word and hoped-for presence of his broken body in the bread and wine and people with HIV. As for prayer, the traditional means of connecting with God, well, that practice was beyond me. There was no true comfort. In a letter to a friend, Flannery O'Connor comes close to expressing the ordeal: "I think there is no suffering greater than what is caused by the doubts of those who want to believe." Add to this distress official disenfranchisement from grace and there is the greater suffering of the discredited gay seeker.

I felt the need for salvation in the present. The daily liturgy during the HIV crisis moderated my unrest by confounding my unbelief, which, I admit, can be as naïve and unexamined as belief. The readings and formal prayers were filled with emotional ambiguity, rough textures, and veiled harmonies. The word *God* carried expectations that the activity of God subverted. Expect a king and find a slave. Trust in an old covenant as absolute and be told it no longer suffices. The messenger of peace invites stoning and gets executed. Jesus upended certainties about life and the Father. For all I knew, that destabilizing effect was scripture's dynamite.

The upshot was uncertainty about faith, naturally, but also about the way I lived my life and conducted my search for nearly fifty years. Prayerful services and academic work were defenses against becoming a brooding outsider. Excusing myself from the crude truth of social involvement came easily. Keeping myself occupied and looking while hiding from God allowed me to escape contact with people. There was another component to being unsociable that AIDS exacerbated. I did not want to face my innately limited capacity for human closeness. I feared my own desire for faith and surely my own desire for God.

The church held an entrenched disregard for the truths of human experience that attests to fluidity in sexual attraction, and it had turned a blind eye to modern science. Medical researchers, for example, have posited an organic basis, both chemical and biological, for sexuality in neurobiological forces that shape complex pathways for erotic desire. Homosexuality is like left-handedness, right-handedness, or ambidexterity. For Christianity to discredit these findings was the Galileo affair again, now battling neuroscience. The distortion of these credible judgments and real-life experience to fit official understanding bespeaks willful dishonesty.

Homophobia, misogyny, un-Christian patriarchy, and moralistic smugness—remnants of creaking institutional rigidities—were very much at work in the church. Those injurious agencies were strikingly at odds with Jesus's own teaching of tolerance that fostered an all-encompassing community. My clash with the church has not been an opposition to God but rather a personal defense of his mysterious creation of human sexual love. Quarrel, then, became a prayer in spite of my disaffection.

Preserving power to buttress the past, I see, has made resistance basic to institutional thinking in society and church. The history of Christianity as an organization has been a history of disagreeable confrontations with new forces at work in era after era. The church is either unable, or unwilling, or scared to deal with the evolving society in which it lives and claims, often loudly, to serve. That dissonance between church teaching and contemporary human knowledge made St. Joseph's an unsteady anchor. Then again, I felt discomfort even in accepting places. (My Fordham office after four decades had nothing personal in it.) As in scripture, discord can serve fruitful moral purposes. In my case, instability and difference of opinion with the church brought me closer to the gospel, which has a healthy skepticism about transient customs passing for lawful absolutes. When the Pharisees protested that the hungry disciples ate grain on the Sabbath, Jesus said,

"I tell you, something greater than the temple is here" (Matthew 12:6). I went to St. Joseph's for that something greater than temple or church.

The physical act of going to church came down to a spiritual act of approaching and avoiding God. Evasions failed to cast out fear and harmed my relations with friends and colleagues and family. I pulled away. Social detachment sharpened my interior unrest and chilled my heart. I was frozen, stuck. My whole being those days was an act for which no word was found. Disenchantment with the church bound me and in time set me free to seek. I knew only that I had to set out on my own to discover whatever would not betray me and scorn me and smash my heart.

2

The Unexpected Moment

He who dwells in friendship dwells in God, and God in him.

—Aelred of Rievaulx, *Spiritual Friendship*

It was a Sunday early afternoon in late August 1981 when I met Frank. He was in New York City for the U.S. Open Tennis Championships in Forest Hills. The outcome of John McEnroe's match with Björn Borg and Tracy Austin's contest against Martina Navrátilová interested me less than did President Ronald Reagan's mid-August appointment of Sandra Day O'Connor to the Supreme Court. Even the elevation of the first woman to the Court, for all its historic importance, however, was a passing concern. I distanced myself, trying especially to keep out the HIV crisis and chaos roaring from the news.

Friends saw through or ignored my defenses. To them I extend belated thanks. A new acquaintance, Terry, called me in the morning. The psychoanalyst we both consulted, who had left New York to work at a psychiatric institute in Sweden, asked Terry to get in touch with me from time to time. Terry phoned this Sunday to say that he was coming down to the Village with a couple of friends who were in the city for the tennis matches in Forest Hills, and they planned to drop by. The call annoyed me. A visit from Terry with a couple of strange men was my idea of invasion.

"I'm not feeling social," I said to Terry's sociable announcement. My voice was cold. Aloof politeness was another way I had of erecting a wall to guard myself. The caller ignored my snootiness. An hour later, he appeared at my door with his boyfriend, Jim, and Jim's friend from college days.

When the three men arrived, I hardly noticed Terry, the man who phoned me, and his boyfriend, except to say hello and to be introduced to their out-of-town visitor. The couple of tall men at the entrance to my apartment were dapper blurs next to the sight of their guest. He was about 5′5″, a bit shorter than I, and stalwart with shoulders rounded by hard work. He had wide brows and sensual lips. His nose seemed to have been broken and imperfectly reset, which added to his brawniness by unbalancing his face. His voice, by contrast, was warm and direct; his mature, super-alive face shone with youthfulness. This stranger's wide *caffé oscuro* eyes, set in a bashful smile with an open manner nabbed me on the spot. Such emotional availability makes and multiplies friends. He extended a muscular stumpy hand with many lines engraving its palm. Frank came into my life.

More than six years of sexual abstinence paradoxically had sensitized me to the real thing. There I was in deep freeze seeking solitude, yet wanting connection. My response was more than sexual. An erotic rush overtook every detail of the moment. This stranger's presence charged me with sudden new delight. My confining billet felt expansive. As sexual need sent me astray into solitude, so physical stirring drew me out to another man. Undesirable desire turned desirable.

When Frank greeted me with a handshake, his blistered right hand reached down to clap something rock-bottom in me. The hand that held me was good, used to work. He was visibly Italian American. His family lived, I soon learned, in the blue-collar Silver Lake section of Belleville, New Jersey, which still had Italian bakeries with brick ovens that made crusty bread and butcher shops that sliced thin veal cutlets to order. Like the Italian immigrant families of my childhood, Frank's neighbors were conservative without having much to be conservative about. All the same, Frank was on happy terms with his ethnicity, the very Old World style and mores that my family had cast off years before.

Frank's body revived that distinctive past in human form. His build of natural shapeliness from physical work reconfigured images of the Italian laborers I had warmed to as a boy. The rope of muscles on Frank's arms reminded me of my strapping grandfather, a machinist for the Pennsylvania Railroad, and of my rugged father, a foreman for several asphalt paving companies. The sound of those distant years also returned in the tricks of Frank's speech. His staccato speaking rhythm was rooted in Essex County; and a New Jersey/New York habit of dropping vowels and the *r* in *park* and *car* occasionally clipped Frank's speech, another mark of his coming from a working-class Italian immigrant family, a mark that my relatives had deliberately shed in favor of slower, "proper" intonations.

Frank's dapper appearance evoked the male style of my Newark childhood days. Appearances mattered to Italians, for whom clothes can be a religion. Back in the '40s (the era of the zoot suit with pegged pants), Italian Americans, even when strapped for money, paid careful attention to clothes as a sign of their self-esteem, despite their low immigrant status. Working-class men wore suits and ties on Sunday and for family picnics. Parents made sure their children dressed well. Feeling that homosexuality lowered his standing even more than his family's foreign origin, Frank refined that habit of stating his self-worth through clothes and developed the fine art of projecting pride, but a pride that was a social emotion, not a moral conceit. Instead of T-shirt and jeans, which were the utilitarian mode I preferred, Frank arrived wearing authentic dark-blue sailor pants with buttons around the front, a white turtleneck shirt, and a blue plaid vest. A gold chain around his neck added a Nicky Newark touch to the Bobby Belleville dash of western boots. This was hardly the uniform of an idea from *GQ*.

Frank wasn't vain, nor was he vamping for attention. In no way shallow or deceitful, he dressed to suit his personal pleasure for an imagined occasion that subtly helped him thrive in adversity. A person with such flair had to be mischievous. He was a fun spirit. I imagined this newcomer as a boy with a freedom to enjoy the playful that I forbade myself. The effect was sexy and soulful. Clothing was for him, I came to understand, one response to overcoming his reserve and the emotional poverty that came with his family's economic hardship. Besides, Frank enjoyed dressing up; it was like trying on various identities, any of which was better than being a deprived gay kid in Belleville.

I naturally compared this dressiness with my practical sense of clothes, which frequently relaxed into scruffiness. One decision settled all matters of dress for me. I liked any color so long as it was blue. Dark gray also passed muster. Shirt and trousers came together simply by my putting them on. Except for when I was teaching, the older and softer the rumpled jeans and shirt, the more I wore them. Indifference allowed me to take my physical existence for granted. I wanted to live in my body without worrying or fussing over it. That's about as far I go in retaining my boyhood.

Natty as was this stranger's outward appearance, something else struck me. His sporty attire was a way of reminding him of his body's value by publicly reclaiming it as his own. I sensed that Frank's sartorial care and my no-frills mode came out at a similar moral place. As gay men, we both sought to protect our bodies from being the object of cultural and ecclesiastical manipulation. Somehow we wanted to say that our bodies belonged to us. Laying claim to our physical selves was a step toward recovering the sexual life forbidden by censorious authorities. Deeper even than our sexual identity, there were, I sensed, life experiences in Frank that bore striking resemblances to my own. There was the price we paid for being gay in blue-collar, New Jersey Italian America and, most crucially, for our thwarted spiritual desires.

Frank's eyes peered into me, as if they found something in me that I had not seen or that perhaps was waiting for detection. Certainly, I beheld in an uninvited guest a readiness for experience that I was trying to tamp down. I was forty-seven and very much in need of the younger man's *joie de vivre*. This grown man at thirty-eight struck me as vitally youthful, not inexperienced so much as having preserved the inner boy, unspoiled. I noticed this boyish energy in baseball players and firemen in their guileless freedom with one another. In Frank I sensed the man-child who was open to the world that said on crossing the threshold of my apartment: Here I am! Let life come!

It must be fun, I thought, to be this man.

Frank's shy smile on meeting me, a total stranger, razed my defenses on the spot. He seemed unscarred by narcissistic skirmishes in the gay *agoras* and raucous after-hours clubs. His moral freshness invited me to be open. Like the desert in the Book of Isaiah that suddenly blossomed, my drab, barren world came into bud. The apartment felt bright and airy. There was life beneath all the layers of fallow self-protection.

No matter how much better Frank made my apartment feel, no matter how fine the energy, I was not prepared to entertain anyone. Nor was I willing—you guessed it—to miss the chance to be with this handsome stranger. And so I proposed that the four of us take a walk. When it came to walking (only walking), I was a closet jock. Lengthy walks not only kept me in what health I had; the physical act invariably buoyed me when my spirits were sinking. I particularly enjoyed moving through the street life of Greenwich Village, where I could be among the city's whirl without having to possess its material wealth or ambition. Pleasure came from living in the neighborhood as a stranger to it all. Just as I am happy when I'm frugal, I like being a stranger, a guest. Because we live in a world not our own, it seems wise to seek rest in the mind and heart of exile.

The numerous trees in the neighborhood made the Village a village. A stroll through its varied, tapered streets induced the feeling of a walk in the park, which had its wild side too. The city trees remained fresh when everyone was drained from HIV/AIDS. Sturdy Japanese elms watched over both sides of Jane Street. They served as arboreal sentries that turned leaving and returning home into a stately affair. Ubiquitous London plane trees with mottled bark, intermittent Norway maples, and random Ginkgos with malodorous seeds and elegant fan-shaped leaves were old pals. On the side streets, pear trees (Bradford Callery variety, I'm told), identifiable by white blossoms announcing spring, pop up here and there. At best, the sundry trunks reached the third or fourth stories of the townhouses, not tall by suburban measure but high enough to whisper to and restore me. Some were scraggly, even during August. All the trees grew lopsided because the sun's presence was oblique, limited by the buildings on the narrow streets.

There was something encouraging to the heart in the irregular shapes of plants that have been left to grow their own way. Humans should be so lucky. On a clear day, if my heart was open to the world,

I could share Isaiah's appreciation that the hand of the Lord has done this, planted in the desert the cedar, acacia, myrtle, and olive.

The four of us walked between the lines of shade trees, all in full bloom on Bleecker Street, the main route of my ambling, which in the 1980s had not yet become a fashion corridor of glitz, and around the West Village, angling toward the Hudson River. Frank's old college friend, who was suffering from the dreaded amoebas that were running through gay men at the time, stopped twice for thick chocolate milkshakes for fast nourishment. I paid attention only to Frank. There was something spry in his step, something alert and gleeful with athletic grace. The throb of compatibility and a fine sexual tension set the pace. We walked along in sync under our own steam. There was a wonderful sense of freedom in feeling young again at forty-seven, in drawing full breath. This new companion and the landscape then came to me as a gift. The present came unannounced and promised to leave me at liberty.

My body was cautiously calling my spirit back to life. Tense years of sexual abstinence and emotional disengagement were slipping away. If my body was susceptible to sickness and death and menaced by the threat of AIDS, my flesh also was responsive to something imperishable in another man, this man.

Frank was almost ten years younger than I. The difference of years between us moved forward to possibility and backward to recovery. From the minute we met, I felt a pull to the childhood I never had in a family rushing to be prosperously American. My immigrant mother in particular did not want her children to waste determining years and energy on unserious matters but to get to the business of preparing for and then carving out a professional space in an educated workforce. That was then; now, in the moment of walking, Frank and I were kids, fresh and free to be ourselves, the spunky Italian boys who used to play stickball and ringolevio on the Newark and Belleville streets.

Our tempo flowed with quick confidences that went straight to the heart. Surprising facts became part of a day of revelation. Frank said that he had been an ordained Catholic priest in a northern New Jersey diocese and had left the ministry. At the time we met, he was working in Morris County, New Jersey, at a Presbyterian chaplaincy council for offenders who needed a high school diploma to change their lives. Like those he was helping, Frank was in transition. He spoke without restraint about living between worlds.

The decision to leave the priesthood wrenched Frank's guts. How could it not? He was at war with himself. Holy orders marked Frank permanently. Every step taken after resignation bore the weight of those vows. He was crossing a moral divide, entering terrain for which there was no map. It hurt staying in the priesthood, and it hurt leaving. Either to his chosen promises or to his true identity, each choice carried the onus of failure. And then there was the impossible ideal of the gospel to which Frank aspired and to which we all fall short. Ordination in the Catholic church made his sexuality a bitter cup. He could not square his awakened need for a meaningful life as a gay man with the chastity required by the official church. Nor would he pretend to be what he was not. Separation from the ministry, which he did not want to be taken from him, made him feel utterly alone, hobbled by past defeat and future misgiving. A heterosexual priest could leave and get married with a dispensation. A gay priest vanishes.

We both led contained lives. Neither of us could get along, go along with the church. I could feel the loneliness in Frank. His loneliness spoke to mine on the frequency of spiritual struggle, which was the only constant in our lives. I was all ears. It was important for Frank to know that someone was really listening. Frank the Jersey boy was more open about himself than I the Village hermit was. Frank's inner life rose quickly to the high point of our conversation. His conflicted feelings emerged spontaneously without a trace of cant, self-pity, or borrowed phrases from television scripts or the therapist's office.

Feeling apart was nothing new to Frank. Before and after ordination he felt cut off. He wanted to be a person for others as a way to being true to himself. Priesthood suggested a way to that goal. With the new openness of the Second Vatican Council (1962–65), life in service to God promised authentic freedom. Like other gay men in his ordination class at St. Mary's Seminary and University in Baltimore,

Frank thought that there was a way for his confreres to reconcile sexuality with the ministry. He could not. Ordination put him under a microscope. He took the truth of his spiritual life and sexuality too seriously to be anything but forthright. Both aspects of his nature demanded an honesty he would not betray.

"Rich," Frank said, rechristening me with a nickname by which I was never addressed but that was welcomed as a sign of this stranger's instant rapport and new identity, "I just couldn't remain a priest and be sexually active and feel true to myself." He risked losing his ministry to find himself. No wonder he dressed so festively. He was eager to shed the trappings of clerical life with its collared suit of armor to reveal the true person.

I had trouble focusing on Frank's inner weakness not only because his body was so strong but also because his self-scrutiny conveyed an acute inner strength. He spoke with a humility that came only from deep self-knowledge. His words passed through his nervous system. That was brave. Acknowledged frailty gave power to what he said. On occasion, I have felt that intensity from others. But Frank's raw passion was piercing. It threatened me with intimacy.

As we walked south down Bleecker Street and crossed Perry Street, I mentioned that Thomas Merton had lived for a while on Perry Street. Merton's spirit was one of many ghosts—his, a benevolent presence—that hang around the neighborhood. Merton's name rang a bell with Frank. He had read Merton's 1948 confessional autobiography, *The Seven Storey Mountain*, which had launched a resurgence of monasticism in the United States after World War II. Frank admired Merton, the restive seeker who gave up his academic career and unsatisfying personal life to become a Catholic and a Trappist monk in the Kentucky hills. Merton's search for a full life began at the same spiritual crossroads where Frank and I found ourselves when we met. Merton felt himself forlorn in the world that was laid waste by boundless materialism and violent aggression, and he sought a refuge from pain and dislocation. Frank and I had also reached the point at which we had to change our lives. Little did we know that the choice involved each other and a sick old woman in a vanilla suburb of New Jersey. But that is jumping ahead.

Though we learned much from Merton about the inner life, Frank and I agreed that his choice of the cloister was not our way to freedom. Gay men did join religious communities, but they lived under the official denunciation of their nature that qualified voluntary acceptance of the rule. Obedience to an institution, to my mind, fostered immaturity through unthinking submission. Monastic life also demanded chastity. Sexual abstention did not work for Frank as a secular priest who worked in the everyday parish setting. As for my experience, well, more than six years of forsaking sexual relations to avoid AIDS had made me miserable and shriveled my soul; I felt like an addict forced into withdrawal pangs. Something about renouncing sex could lead to unlovingness, both the inability to love and to be loved by others.

Merton's appeal, we agreed, was his understanding that the longing for the spring of life was in every person and that everyone had the talent, to greater or lesser degree, to undertake the search for the fullness of life. Merton's writing consistently honors those who follow the truth with all the sincerity of their conscience. He is the brother of those who have no trust, who drink the wine of sorrow, and who gather in exile. Looking back on our meeting, I recognize another aspect of Merton's life that affected Frank and me. With Merton, God's grace to conversion came through friends who shared his confusion and isolation. The power of friendship was beginning to operate in the two of us lost Jersey boys, fully grown, walking that late August day.

We wandered, Frank bearing his past and I bearing with him as confidant. He recalled three years of pre-seminary study of Greek and Latin at Seton Hall University that were academic drudgery and personally repressive for him. The clerical atmosphere was tense. The priests of the Newark Archdiocese in charge of the pre-seminary program were like members of the rules committee of a pretentious men's club. They watched over the divinity students as sneaky enforcers of an unstated code. Their power came from making the younger men feel that they were being judged and found academically and spiritually wanting. The priests were also hurtful with one another. They made a point of ostracizing one of their number who was gay by not sitting with him at dinner. Frank couldn't wait to move on.

The next two years of philosophy at St. Mary's Seminary and University in Baltimore for a B.A. in 1969, followed by four years of theology leading to an M. Div. in 1973 required sustained effort from Frank; but here the residential academic setting engendered a feeling of community, purpose, and support among the students. Studying theology, especially scripture, in the wake of the Vatican Council happily encouraged debate about decrees and engagement with Protestants and Jews. A spirit of ecumenical excitement instilled the soul of Catholicism with moral freshness, the very vitality of the gospel that the institution had neglected in favor of political power.

Intellectual expansion enhanced personal relations among young seminarians. The daily round of liturgy and communal prayers made for a mutually respectful life. The feeling of emotional liberty came from the Sulpician fathers, members of a French order known for its scholarship, who ran St. Mary's with personal concern for the students' spiritual welfare. "At best, I was an average student," Frank said, "but I tried to accept my limitations without putting myself down." Above all, the seminary got him away from his family so that he could see himself by light of a wider community. "They were good days," he said. Like all good days, they were the first to flee.

The best part of the late 1960s and early 1970s for progressive Catholics was the spirit of *aggiornamento*, or institutional updating of its closed medieval mindset to embrace the contemporary condition. The Second Vatican Council's call for renewal held out hope to gay seminarians. They saw the church's regard for the modern experience and scientific understanding of homosexuality as opening a way for them to cast off the disguises that bound gay believers. Could a person just be Catholic without being a gay or straight Catholic, a bad or good Catholic? It didn't seem foolhardy at the time to hope that sweeping reforms would recognize the entire range of human sexuality as sacred. After all, it was God who created the continuum of sexual desire.

One advantage of studying at St. Mary's in Baltimore for Frank was the training he received at Johns Hopkins for hospital ministry. Helping the sick and dying put flesh on textbook theology and spiritual ideals. Being gay would not come between Frank, the wounded healer, and those needing to be healed. Rather, the hurt of homosexuality would bring him closer to their suffering. If clerical authority intimidated Frank, his being at the axis of life and death with the sick affirmed him. He knew something about discussing hurtful matters that others avoided. There seemed, then, to be a job for Frank in God's plan. So far, so good. One can, after all, find God everywhere. Furthermore, many gay men at the time thrived in their parish work. The air of change encouraged the naïve assumption that these gay priests could lead an honest life that the church would come around to accept.

Like Frank's professional development, his inner progress went unevenly. His deaconate, a year before final vows, was spent in a small Italian American parish in Paterson, New Jersey. *Deacon* comes from the Greek (*diakonos*) for the ordained office of servant related to priesthood that, by the way, in the early centuries included women and men. Here at the parish, hard facts of ordained service burst the seminary bubble of collegiality and idealism. Unlike Franciscans or Dominicans, diocesan priests had neither an order nor a committed brotherhood to fall back on. Most parish priests were overworked, and many had trouble making their own financial ends meet. Each was economically responsible for his own retirement, whereas religious orders took care of their own unto death. Even ascetic Trappists and eremitic Carthusians enjoyed more fraternal support than did secular priests. Parish life could be lonelier than a charterhouse cell or Cistercian monastery. Left on their own, diocesan priests could not help but take on the basic instincts instilled by the competitive world they served. As a result, politics and power encroached upon mutual support.

The time as deacon was a year-long rite of passage meant to prepare a young man for parish life, and so it did for Frank. Great. The experience introduced him to what it was like to occupy a rung of social forbearance somewhere between tolerated guest and enemy combatant in the disciplinary setup of boot camp for aspiring assistant curates. As a deacon, Frank had a windowless room without a bath. Dearth of light and space set the terms of the regimen. Dignity went the way of privacy. The pastor was a drill sergeant for basic training of religious recruits. Frank was the pastor's janitor and gofer, fixing the electric light panel and making coffee for a prayer group into which he was not invited.

It was not the menial jobs or the large number of them that riled Frank. It was being pushed around by his desire to serve God that got to him. God's will was invoked to keep one down. As Frank put it with self-accepting, farsighted humor, "I sat at the kids' table." Later he supervised the altar boys (no girls were altar servers) for whom he chartered buses to attend the Mets and Yankees games.

Ordination in May 1974 immersed Frank deeper in the inevitable struggles with human insufficiencies, both his and those of the institution. The gospel can disappear in daily personal exchanges. When Frank asked the pastor if he could use the church basement to invite his family and friends for dinner after his first Mass, the pastor denied him. Happily, the nearby Syrian church provided the space that Frank's own pastor refused him. The handsome young priest threatened the old one. The gentleness that the pastor mocked in Frank endeared him to the parishioners, who were better judges of character and were stronger advocates for change. His affection for people, it seemed, came from his deep inner loneliness.

The diocese's personnel director, recognizing that Frank was easy to get along with, assigned him to a pastor who couldn't handle a strong, independent assistant. Weakness, however, lived off weakness. A new and guileless young priest made for an easy target. Frank's doubts about himself magnified his vulnerability and resulting pain. What he found were superiors who lacked confidence and simple kindness. For the pastor to feel strong, Frank had to be more dependent and unhappier than he was. Transferring his cowardice and addiction onto the nearest mark, the pastor falsely accused Frank of being an alcoholic requiring treatment. The older priest relieved his loneliness by constructing a catch-22: Frank's denial of addiction amounted to a confirmation that he was an alcoholic.

A new assignment on the fringe of the Paterson diocese brought different tensions with the pastor and fellow priests. Frank's mild temperament helped and hurt him. His gentleness united Frank with his parishioners. That popularity made the pastor envious and the situation more alienating. Power plays overrode the importance of the sacraments. Parish life for Frank offered only different and heavier burdens, not a relief from self-doubt. Frank, by his lights, lacked the strength of grace to find himself faithful. Parish life was a shell game with the pretension of doing God's work as the cover for living by one's own will for one's gain. He had to suck up authoritarianism.

Gender relations were problematic. One pastor with whom Frank worked dealt with his attraction to women by being bossy and argumentative to keep them at a safe distance. He confused and hurt the women he sought out. "His weakness," Frank remarked with sympathy for all the parties involved, "was the women's pain of rejection with no explanation." Gay or straight, sexuality distorted by repression got in the way of ministering to others. The desire to serve God led Frank to and out of ordination. He had sought a place, a life, unencumbered by institutional hypocrisy where his best self could freely help others. But that was not to be in official ministry. The conflict between homosexuality and religious desire left Frank feeling burnt out. He was so young—early thirties—and so disillusioned. And yet I felt in him a still-youthful vitality ready for a true ministry to call upon him. He would have to look elsewhere to find his soul. It's a matter of losing one's way to find one's center.

At thirty-eight, just beyond the middle of his life with virtually no material resources, Frank embodied an austere perspective. Behind him was the hard and meek path of having worked since he was eight in his grandfather's grocery store; ahead loomed an uncharted world. Yet Frank was not anxious. By nature he had renounced the professional and monetary securities that drive us only to fail us. Frank was also without a trace of entitlement of any kind. He gave off not even a hint of the sexual claim that usually accompanied his buff Italian good looks.

Many of the difficulties and rivalries that Frank mentioned, though not his emotional responses, struck me as small stuff, the abrasions that make up the give-and-take in any professional life. Just at the point of seeming to present himself as the victim, Frank paused and looked down at the pavement. "I know I was hypersensitive and felt mocked when I wasn't, excluded when I didn't get the extra attention

I wanted. Looking back, I see that I wasn't ready for priestly work. I was naïve. I needed very basic reassurances of my worth."

The problem was neither in Frank's character nor in his desire for personal holiness but in the direction he had taken toward finding his true self through serving others. The office emanating from the altar was one way but not the only way. A change in direction did not mean a change in calling. Nor would a new life necessitate disowning his true self, which was irrevocably gay. After several floundering years, this radical awareness of a human vocation outside the official church was apparently, tentatively, taking hold in Frank. The poverty, dejection, inadequacy, and sinfulness that Frank felt personally suited him to serve the people of God at the side of a hospital bed or in the unexpected moment of another person's anguish. But such a self-appreciation takes time, if it ever comes. The starting point was in the way his intuitive trust in me brought me close to him. He dared to reveal to me the heartrending truths of his thwarted spiritual desires in the ministry.

Frank's openness and modesty were not a mask for pride. Plumbing his inner life didn't prevent Frank from reaching out to others. The candor behind his reciting his unworthiness suggested the capacity not to be afraid of any painful truth about himself. Such fearlessness served Frank well some years later when he was diagnosed with Parkinson's disease that froze his agile hands and then underwent radiation for prostate cancer at Memorial Sloan-Kettering. During all nine weeks of radiation, Frank made a point of going to work every day and then leaving alone to keep the treatment from becoming a big deal that took over his life. Frank responded with more than usual acceptance to both life-changing diseases. "It is what it is," he said. His unblinking eye was the viewpoint of faith in life itself. He seemed unflappable, not to say impossibly considerate of other people, especially me. But that's getting far ahead of the story.

When we first met, Frank's ruthless self-scrutiny awakened something deep in my heart. It was consistent with Frank's integrity that he retold situations of rejection that hurt him. Such courage is rare and probably comes about only when facing out one's entire biography in the company of God's mercy. Strength born of lowliness struck me as a sign of genuine spiritual power. I wondered about such humility because I actually lacked even simple expressions of the virtue. But I felt the power of genuine humility when it came my way. Frank did not share my trust in self-reliance or see personal accomplishments as the basis for contentment or good fortune. Such healthy skepticism about these illusory strengths protected him against some of the inner trickeries of pride that duped me. I wanted to escape into the friendship that this man's sincerity presaged. He had a natural emotional intelligence.

Frank had a sense of humor to go with his self-awareness. With a knowing smile, he recalled how his parents argued about leaving dirty dishes in the sink instead of dealing with the real troubles between them. "I couldn't handle the big problems either, and so I responded to the small. Feeling hurt stopped me from looking inside." His voice had gentleness and power—an all but impossible combination.

Where did this man come from?

Frank and I were different, very different; and yet his inner conflicts raised questions in my own thoughts about how homosexuality bears on spiritual aspiration. Being gay and seeking God are inextricably bound at the generative vortex of one's nature. As I wondered about the forces that shaped Frank, he became a mystery to me, one that has deepened with time.

Homosexuality alone did not impede Frank. His lifelong struggle with inner barrenness left him weak and susceptible to prescribed ways to a virtuous identity. "I studied for the priesthood because I wanted to serve people and to develop an inner life by working for others. At first, it didn't seem to me that being gay was incompatible with being a priest," Frank said. "Before I could do any serious spiritual work, I have to do serious psychological work. That's where I am right now." He had been seeking guidance from a Presbyterian minister trained in counseling. "I need to turn my life around," he said. "I'm stuck and don't to want be. I want to move Godward." He was engaging with his demons, with his and everyone's search for God. His openness turned me into a spiritual sidekick. But again, I'm jumping ahead of the story.

Frank poured his heart out—but this exposure to a virtual stranger? Had I known, I would have packed a big lunch for two. He was more naked than any stripped lover in bed. Such self-baring, conceivably, arose from being socially shy. Whatever the origin, he generated an air of affecting release that I needed most. My new companion's openness was really his extending the grace of trust, which invited me, innately wary and doubting, to respond with corresponding trust in him. For the first time in my life, I wanted someone—this man—to know me.

Along with this blessing, Frank's predicament put before me the question, Who said that you can't serve God if you are gay? Not the Greek Bible. Certainly not Jesus, who seemed comfortable with the sexuality of others. I didn't for a minute ever believe that the creator of life sanctioned only heterosexuality to do God's work any more than the universal God of scripture empowered one gender over another or one culture over another.

Far from being an impediment to seeking God, being gay had to set the terms for Frank's new direction. That was unavoidable. Becoming faithful to God required loyalty to his God-given sexuality. Frank's pursuit of an integrated life expressed my desire for a fuller life. Cut adrift and deprived of support, we were both casting about in a void for the fullness that answered to the will of God. We would be our best by being what God made us to be, but gay men and lesbians had nowhere in the church to spend our courage. In describing Frank's predicament, I am of course expressing my spiritual impasse. To feel the shared impasse was to sense how a human relation opens the way out to trust in God. One follows the other as day follows night.

But how does living by the inescapable truth of one's homosexuality dispose one to God's will when Christianity had made homosexuality an affliction? Frank and I knew we were on our own—until we met—with no institutional church providing for us. The attraction he and I shared would set us on a course that disproved certain assumptions that I didn't know I held. Not usually lost for words, I could not even suppose how to express the spirituality of same-sex love, given that the vocabulary had been co-opted and denigrated by church teaching. In high school, teachers of religion drummed into us that homosexuality was a perversity against nature. A 1986 letter from the

Congregation for the Doctrine of the Faith, then led by the current Pope Benedict XVI, declared homosexuality a "more or less strong tendency toward an intrinsic moral evil." In the words of contemporary hierarchal jargon, homosexuality is "objectively disordered."

Besides supplying a benediction for oppression, ecclesiastical contempt assails the intrinsic nature of a gay person: in the ability to trust, to love others, and in the capacity to have a faith in God. By turning mere fickle cultural attitudes into moral absolutes, religion stunts spiritual growth. Managing the inner damage on a gay person parallels coping with HIV infection. As the retrovirus cannot be eradicated from the body, only controlled, the trauma of early assault on the gay psyche remains unhealed, though friends, time, and self-awareness do make living with the gay stigma easier. The gospel also helps. The good news not only proclaims love but also embodies its practice in true flesh. Far from condemning homosexuality, Jesus takes great risks to state publicly the inclusiveness of God's compassion. His message of course comes to us when we are ready to hear it. When I met Frank, I was learning anew to listen to the good news.

I wish that as a gay teenager looking for guidance I had grasped Luke's account (4:16–30) of Jesus's being hounded out of his birthplace by his own people. It's an unsentimental story of the timeless human need to survive public hate. Jesus comes to the synagogue in Nazareth, his third visit home, to worship and, as is his custom, to deliver his message there. His news on this occasion concerns God's favor reaching beyond Judaism. To that end, Jesus reminds the Nazarenes that Israel has rejected Elijah's help, whereas foreigners are more disposed to God's aid. Jesus's comparison aims to unlock the sealed religious mind that restricts God to its proprietary self-interest. Though Gentiles and lepers may not seem to the Pharisees as worthy as Jews, the open trust of outsiders recommends these non-Jews to God. In turn, God's mercy has chosen them as his own. The magnitude of the message hits home. Jesus's call for inclusion infuriates the self-entitled Nazarenes. "And they rose up and put him out of the city, and led him to the brow of the hill on which their town was built, that they might hurl him down headlong. But passing through the midst of them he went away" (Luke 4:29–30).

Despite their murderous intent, the Nazarenes do not molest Jesus. Nor does Luke account for Jesus's safe crossing. Conventional piety might see a miracle at work here, and leave it at that. Textual critics with an eye to harmonic narrative design say that Jesus's time had not yet come. Fair enough, if disembodied agencies satisfy one's understanding of God's presence. For me there is more to the living God. In fact, far from illusory, God's nearness is a tremendous reality. His enfleshed power takes the form of human dignity that physically guards Jesus. If fear attracts danger, self-belief deters it. Jesus knows who he is and whose word he delivers. Those with ears to hear do respond to his truth. People "were astonished at his teaching, for his word was with authority" (Luke 4:32).

As Jesus teaches, so he walks. His movement maps the possibilities of hope for those whom society hunts down. Dignity keeps Jesus safe not only from inner harm but also from the zealots' assault on his personal liberty. This unseen armor protects Jesus as he travels through Judea. Subsequently when Jesus goes to Jerusalem for the Jewish feast of Tabernacles, his enemies "sought to arrest him; but no one laid hands on him" (John 10:30). So Jesus escapes the enemies' hands equipped to stone him.

The Pharisaic threat lives on in Christianity with the identical aim to exclude and injure. With hundreds of millions of gay people on the planet, judging homosexuality as psychological derangement further amounts to an indictment of gross divine blunder. Deemed as a blight on the soul, being gay forced me to consider the association to the Absolute that others might take for granted. Am I beyond the cross? Does not the crucifixion embrace the totality of human experience? Going back over our fundamental link to God cannot but help homosexuals recover their rightful, full nature. If we think of our humanness in the unfathomable scheme of creation as an honor, might being gay also be a privileged way to escape the confines of orthodoxy? That struggle, on balance, is the founding drama of Jesus's saving life.

Frank and I, strays that we were, met as strangers and parted as secret sharers who fathomed each other's bewilderment and private methods for living as gay men amid moral self-doubt and desolation. By the magnetic needle of instinctive trust, we roamed the inner and outer places of loneliness. The alarm of AIDS encircling us on the streets beset our encounter. The day darkened. The swirl of Greenwich Village life stopped spinning for a few moments. Frank and I stood in relief against the suspended activity and danger. I settled for the sheer delight of stumbling upon a stranger who seemed unstrange. It was a triumph over self-sabotage, a step toward overcoming a crippling past.

Our excursion ended by circling back past Jane Street to the subway station at 14th Street and Eighth Avenue. Frank was leaving with Terry and Jim to get his car, parked in a garage on the Upper West Side near Jim's building, to return to the suburban New Jersey house that two former parishioners had lent him until he could find his own place. We locked eyes. I committed Frank's face to memory. He became formal, a bit shy. I don't recall shaking his hand when we parted. That gesture would have been too proper for the confidences that had passed between us, just as embracing would have been too showy and presumptuous for a first encounter of two diffident men. Frank and I acknowledged the day by exchanging phone numbers before Frank in turtlenecked aloneness went off to his New Jersey desert, and I in T-shirted solitude withdrew to the lockdown of my own making on Jane Street.

The Sunday walk was a chance crossing of two nomads, three if we included Merton's shadow, and four if we acknowledged the giver of grace who oversaw the happy meeting in the first place. These courtesies converged to found a first acquaintanceship with a soft nod to our hidden selves. As long it was, the walk was a mere preliminary to go further inward off the beaten path.

My memory of that Sunday in late August remains anchored in a vivid picture. Toward evening, Frank and I watched the sea gulls in the homeless sky over the Hudson. The birds were flying smoothly in accompaniment to our walk. They were free in wind and wave with the ability to ride smooth and rough weather by going with the tide. Eventually, when a certain season comes, they must go back to a locale they have known—to a secluded island or forlorn ridge that was the ground of their being.

The turmoil of youth, I believe, has such a shelter. Unaccountably, with all the unprecedented fortune of our accidental meeting, the gray and snowy creatures with long wings curving in descent along the Manhattan waterfront gave Frank and me courage. On separate currents of the same atavistic flow coming from cramped formative years as gay boys in the Italian-American world of northern New Jersey, the two of us seemed headed to such a place, even though we may have been afraid of it.

3

This is what really matters most of all to everyone: the power
to be made new.

—*The Reed of God*, Caryll Houselander

In mid-September 1981, several weeks after we met, Frank came to
Greenwich Village on a late Saturday morning. It was a date, our first
date, if just hanging around my apartment qualifies as an appointment
between two persons seeking the affections of each other. After embracing like old friends, we made love like gawky kids. Frank's body
was marble. No fireworks. Just feeling around the dips and curves of
each other's muscles for the sinews within to experience the pulsing
life of invisible affection.

We knew that we were placing more hope in the body than flesh
could hold. Nonetheless we got great pleasure from reclaiming our
bodies from neglect. Smiles and unabashed laughter lifted us from
good feeling to better feeling. Frank's desires, quiet, odors were filling
me up. The scent of my new friend was the smell of a new field that
had received blessing at its roots. I soaked up his sensual presence.
There was no walking around the Village this time. We didn't leave
the apartment. We didn't have to. We felt as complete as two solitudes
joining without knowing what we were in for. Frank stayed overnight
until early Sunday evening.

After this first intimate time together, I phoned Frank now and
again. The ease that we felt previously at my place was not in the
conversation. Formality shaped his voice. He was at the very least

keeping a distance from the implications of the visit. I was baffled. He didn't strike me as a man who played games. It was as if we hadn't been naked with each other. Or had our actual nakedness spoiled for Frank the grand emotions of the first encounter during which we talked about spiritual matters? Perhaps he was confronting the mutable relationship of our bodies. He gave no clue. His reserve was a punch in the gut. Stuck in sexual adolescence, I savored feeling hurt. His avoiding me tore open my insecurities. Something was going on with Frank, and I read his holding back by my own selfishness. Being rejected gave me the upper moral hand and a reason to withdraw to my default mode of solitude.

I doubted that having sex with another man was the problem for him. The carbon from a one-night stand or hit-and-run test drive, if that was all the weekend was for him, wouldn't stay long in his lungs. But if he had invested the unlived life that I had put into our sexual intimacy, that would have been another matter. Then he would have to come out from the shadows to acknowledge that he is a man who loves men. Self-acceptance changes everything. The admission would have given the weekend a future at the same time that it opened him to public repudiation. For whatever cause, Frank was stressed out. That much I knew.

My phone calls put the untimely pressure of my needy emotions on him. The closeness that I was ready for, or thought I was, may have alarmed Frank, and for good reasons that I was too erotically impatient to consider. Protecting himself made sense. Getting hurt and the possibility that the other person might move on weighed heavily on a sensitive man recently out of the ministry. Frank needed calm stability rather than the tension of courtship with the discomfiting intimacy of a possible affair. He was now gay by desire and act. And in a state of compulsory silence, self-acknowledgment is an act of resistance.

Excitement got the best of me. Living alone can make everyone else a minor character in the soap opera of one's private romantic narrative. All I wanted was to get out of the trap I set for myself. Selfishness triggered in me a readiness easily to give and take offense. This was an old fault I had difficulty breaking. Wanting to know Frank better gave me the courage to manage the turmoil caused by physical desire.

Frank was less knee-jerk. After years of dealing with parishioners' unhappiness and his own conflicted soul, he was more circumspect. Nothing was ever given to him. He had to work for everything, especially love. Though nine years younger than I, Frank had developed an emotional caution that I lacked. That discretion heightened my eagerness to be with him. His pulling away actually showed how much our making love meant to him. He may also have sensed a truth that I hid from myself. I was afraid to trust myself with anyone. We both felt the power of liberating (and dangerous) desire.

Nearly a month later, Frank returned to Manhattan. I tried to respond to his healthy reserve. Picking up on my self-conscious cool, he humored me. I never learned how to be comfortable with someone when erotic desire was in the air. Frank's boyish sense of the casual softened my mannered stuffiness. Light-heartedness made him the kind of person one just wanted to hang out with. He came for the afternoon and stayed for dinner and the night until Sunday afternoon. If there were no grand moments during this weekend, there were hints of the homey feelings that would be the great proportions of our bond. We eventually called such uneventful passages our Ma-and-Pa evenings, the high watermark to which our emotions rose.

His Manhattan visit set a courting pattern for Saturday and Sunday. This new man in my life was also getting me into physical and emotional shape. We jogged down the West Side Highway until I got a heel spur. We took walks, which were very much a part of my pleasure in city street-life. The days centered on being in each other's company. We were two men with ingrained habits of caution that could be taxing and, in retrospect, comical. As façades fell, we regressed back to boyish enthusiasms. Often Frank called me "kid." Despite his being younger, the nickname was his way of filling in for the childhood he believed I never had. Fortunately, my self-consciousness dissolved in the round of domestic doings.

From the first, breaking bread was crucial to our learning about each other. Our Italian upbringing left us with similar tastes in food and a shared a sense of its importance in drawing people together. We spent Saturday afternoons at the big outdoor Union Square greenmarket. The excursion of ten blocks from Jane Street to the heart of country in the heart of city was a high for the palate. We roamed from booth to booth to sample hot pretzels, fresh organic cheese, and apple slices that never saw cold storage. A snacking tour hardly rivaled breakfast at Tiffany's, but it was falling in love in New York—1980s style, surrounded by HIV ruins. Along the way, Frank usually stopped to buy flowers. His extravagance never rubbed on me. Flowers struck me as costly reminders of life's transience. Our main purpose was to buy food for supper. Making the day was our day. It unfolded through a geometry of expectancy and surprise at the table.

In the evening, simple food confirmed the relaxed feelings leading up to the meal. Just being together for salad and pasta gave newness to old flavors. *Mezze penne* with tomato sauce and topped with ricotta and fresh basil, a dependable standby, never tasted so good. A future with a friend was in the very flavor of the food of memory, in the goodness. Breaking bread was another way of breaking our loneliness in two.

From the start, I sensed that I had taken up with a homebody who was the classic good influence. After dinner, it did not occur to us to go to a gay bar. The boozing world of public smiles and clubbing finesse was a scene in which I, at best generic in appearance, never had the looks or style to compete. Frank had the looks but not the knack. In the main, the bar ambiance promoted a masculinity defined by chiseled bodies and attitudes developed past being attractive. Besides, I didn't drink, and Frank enjoyed lying on the sofa watching a movie or reading while getting his feet massaged. Sheltering intimacy filled the bill.

Simple domesticity was tangibly remaking the self I devised in order to stave off contact with my true self that was buried beneath fear and resentment. Touch by natural touch, the passionate part of me that was ashamed to live out in the open was coming out of hiding. I had the feeling of being in the presence of new measures. The lure was to a different scale of relations. Our need for God was both explicitly discussed and subtext. In the exchanges and living our interest in each other, Frank was teaching me that we gain the spiritual by exploration of the physical, sexuality included. In this school for sacramental knowledge I count myself a slow learner.

It did not take long to experience Frank's generosity. On his third or fourth visit, he stopped at his family's house in Belleville, New Jersey, on Saturday morning for a container of his mother's homemade sausage and meatball gravy, which neither of our families ever called sauce, just as they always referred to pasta as macaroni. Our weekend ended after we watched the Sunday episode of the PBS television presentation of Evelyn Waugh's *Brideshead Revisited*. This eleven-week tuxedoed exploration of homoerotic desire mangled by Roman Catholicism supplied an amusing, if poignant, backdrop for our blue-collar magnetism.

When Frank left for New Jersey, I pulled things together for Monday classes. Every Sunday around ten o'clock, we called each other to extend the enjoyment of the weekend. For years, the ring of the phone bothered me. Even messages of solicitude and kindness came as unwanted intrusions or signaled a medical problem with my mother; but with Frank usually at the other end, the telephone became eventful. I was glad to hear Frank's voice whether he called here in Manhattan or there in New Jersey. The ring grabbed me with the gladness of hearing Frank's New Jersey voice. The call was the topic. We talked just to hear the other speak. Voice linked our interior worlds. This was the first time in my life that I, a cheapskate, wasn't concerned about long-distance charges on the monthly bill.

Having met in the middle of personal crises, we spent time filling in our back-stories. Frank was expansive about his life; I was more guarded. The terrified gay kid in me—still vying with the tested forty-seven-year-old—did not want anyone to know him. I even held back with this new man who was trying to make me happy. I needed secrecy for friendship, and distance for affection. When the conversation turned to Catholicism, as it often did, Frank was candid about his trust in God. I was cagey about what I sought and held true.

Sometimes I thought of God as an extraordinary being among other beings; sometimes, as the source of life beyond all beings; sometimes, as a gap. Most of the time, I tried not to pay any attention to God. I was incredulous. The plain fact that the word *God* existed troubled me. The word had neither shape nor reality. I had no experience whatever of the divine. I needed to experience God as I did a tree or another human being. Without direct contact, I was lost. Faith based in doctrinal technicalities was wasted on me. Nonetheless, the word *God* outlasted my dilemma with it, and my protests contributed to the word's power. Keeping silent was futile. In the language of society, talk about God would never cease. I left Frank to deal with God on his own and listened. I stayed with the details of how I got to where I was in the present.

My emotional energy, I explained to my new, dear friend, centered on my mentally stricken mother. She lived with my unmarried sister, Marie, in Cedar Grove, a postwar suburban New Jersey hamlet about twenty miles across the Hudson. Marie taught high school and for her personal good continued to work. By the early 1980s, my mother's slow mental decline from an unknown cause called for regular though not constant attention. I provided company for them. My job was to make sure that our mother had dressed and eaten and to reassure Marie while at work that our mother was safe and sound.

My renewed relations with the two women, as with meeting Frank, happened by chance, and against my will. Both my mother and sister were strong women. Italian tradition endowed their love with generous affection that got hold of you and would not let you go. No matter where I lived and whatever my work, my being unmarried meant I was under familial care and jurisdiction. I linked their loyalty, probably unfairly, to the conformist culture of the era and place. As a gay teenager growing up in Essex County in northern New Jersey, I couldn't wait to get away from its homophobia and many cultural constraints of small town with sensible structures in the shadow of New York. I assumed that I would stay away, far away. Family meant little to me. That split-level home, where at best I felt like a visitor, was not my true home, until it was years later.

Needing a break from graduate study, I landed an instructorship at Notre Dame. I took the job for what I thought would be a year of renunciation that turned into a nine-year hitch, with a year off in Italy on a Fulbright fellowship. Notre Dame afforded an opportunity to grow professionally, and northern Indiana opportunely put more than 700 miles between my family and me. South Bend was a buckhorn grass prairie. Its French heritage and Potawatomi Indians were no-where in sight. Not yet even a quasi–college town, South Bend in 1958 was a small city of declining industrial enterprises such as Studebaker-Packard, Singer, and Bendix. The provincialism held only frustration for a gay man in his late twenties aching for a genuine life beyond that of a traditionalist homosocial Catholic university. (Women were not admitted to Our Lady's University until 1972.) Because mythologized manhood went with the school's carefully groomed image of post–World War II virility, a gay man had to tread softly through potential shame, both feeling exposure and causing it. In the classroom and with some colleagues, a gay instructor could feel integral to the university; but because of the criminalized status of homosexuality, he essentially lived in isolation. I tried but couldn't drown my displacement in work.

Before the legendary Stonewall Rebellion in 1968 that incited the gay rights movement, the battle for a gay man was against taking on the pathologized interpretation of homosexuality that intertwined with religious bigotry. I lived in a confused culture that affirmed my teaching and scholarship while denigrating my sexual identity. I had heard of a gay bar in South Bend called the Jolly Spot on Jefferson Avenue (Jefferson Boulevard?), but in my nine years at Notre Dame I didn't dare go there to meet other men. Dissembling, then, unavoidably shaped my life. The seedy Greyhound Bus station was the main cruising ground. There one hid the obvious purpose for checking out the scene. One especially kept secret the evident fact that one was both gay and connected with the university. Sex was furtive and vexed by town/gown misgivings. I inhabited an underground within an under-ground. To be gay was to lead a secretive, parochial life in a parallel universe of repression. When I went to nearby Chicago, the region's Mecca for gay people, I felt like a hick.

Teaching was rewarding, and I was young enough to be on friendly terms with students, especially the fifth-year architects, an arty (for Notre Dame) and freewheeling cadre, who took my class studying short stories. I was not unhappy; nor was I happy. I was resigned to a limited life and an uneventful career. At least I thought that I had made peace with a professional situation that forced gay people into denial. But something within me rebelled against containment and invisibility. What flared up was a glib hauteur to compensate for and to rise above the cultural and personal forces tamping me down. I shot myself in the foot. My self-importance played into departmental politics. As a result, I made enemies when I didn't need to or want to. My contract was not renewed. I left in disappointment, not with Notre Dame but with myself. I couldn't accept affirmation on the terms with which it was given. In the end, my path, favorably, steered through Notre Dame, but it also, favorably, steered me away from it. Departure from a place that had been so professionally formative was a bit like being turned out from Eden. But as with the eviction from the Garden, a more conflicted and fuller life was in store.

Colleges and universities in the late 1960s needed new faculty for the burgeoning student population, and the lower birthrate during the mid-1930s made for few Ph.D.s in the job market. Demographics were on my side. For young scholars with publications, the academy was an expanding universe. Offers came through. In 1966, Fordham University was well thought of and interested in hiring me. Because my first book—a study of Willa Cather's use of music—was coming out, the position came with a promotion to associate professor. I snatched the offer.

Cities befriend gay people; they welcome and look the other way. I was thirty-two and ready for a big city, especially New York, the archipelago of liberty. Though just across the Hudson River from my family, Manhattan was a world elsewhere, one where I could inhale long breath and live as openly as the times permitted. I imagined that behind the city's screen of green trees and skyscrapers all New York lay at my feet. And in 1966 the Metropolitan Opera opened a new house at Lincoln Center. Great music was an extra incentive. Attending the opera was like going to the liturgy. During the overture I enjoyed settling back in a family circle seat to let great voices from around the world lift me into their sky-piercing arias and cadenzas. Living in Manhattan meant I wouldn't have to trek ninety bleak miles to hear and the Lyric Opera of Chicago and the Chicago Symphony. I could take a subway to hear the renowned Herbert von Karajan debut conducting *Die Walküre* the next season. I did. A new power of change was in the air around me as Wagner's gods were being schooled in human love and politics.

Political awakening came with moving to Manhattan in 1967. Though I was a child of the inhibited generation of the 1930s that grew up in the complacent 1950s, I didn't come of age until I got to New York in the late 1960s. Everything at that time was speeding up, as mind-altering drugs were hurling consciousness into overdrive. Vietnam, Martin Luther King Jr., the women's movement, civil rights, and the experimental theater were all charging the city's atmosphere with intellectual excitement. The first time I went to the Caffe Cino on Carmine Street, I was shocked to hear unleashed the strident rhetoric of anti-government protest. Hearing President Lyndon Johnson called a murderer stunned me. I was taught to uphold the status quo all the while the existing condition held me down. Avant-garde playwrights were jolting audiences out of political and dramatic complacency by tearing into our government for its deceit and unconscionable violence in a brutalizing war in Vietnamese villages.

The release of raw feelings exhilarated me. Even though the ripping language would never comfortably fit my more restrained voice, such fighting words expressed my views about the country's exercise of power. The fledgling Radical Gay Caucus and Gay Liberation sponsored consciousness-raising groups based on the widespread feminist meetings. For three years I met with such a group. The collective discussions opened my eyes to the way politics affected the most intimate human experiences, not excluding religious belief. I felt as much at home in countercultural Manhattan as I would anywhere, which still left plenty of room for feeling out of the mix.

No doubt about it, in starting a new life amid the wide freedoms of cosmopolitan New York, I hit the gap between school and career. The resources of New York helped me to fill the disparity. What I heard and saw on the streets and in underground spaces summoned me to find a place in the world. I was an associate professor in my early thirties and felt politically like an undergraduate freshman.

Through Jean-Claude van Itallie from the gay consciousness-raising group, I fell in with a number of writers, directors, and actors working in The Living Theater and The Open Theater. These two radical performance groups sought to change the theater from its moribund commercial restrictions to accommodate the radical political reforms necessitated by governmental deceit and violence institutionalized by the Vietnam War. In the Marxist style of Bertolt Brecht, the actors were the audience in the act of changing public and personal life through art. The questions of acting in this new theater dealt directly with acting in life on behalf of exposing and uprooting of injustice. That aesthetic strategy opened my eyes to the fact that literature looked beyond the library carrels where I was sequestered.

The aesthetic made new ethical statements about minorities, women, and gay rights. They stood with those who refused to serve in Vietnam—refused, that is, to kill. Many members of the performance groups were arrested and jailed for their beliefs. The directors and actors' resistance to war and commitment to social justice gave me permission to acknowledge my own sluggish progressive loyalties. These principled ideals came with a concern for the varieties of spiritual journeys anchoring political life. Religion, so central to the struggle of the Jews in these groups, called for political action. Their work drew from an intense personal involvement in how inner life molds social action.

When Joe Chaikin and Jean-Claude van Itallie, director and playwright, respectively, of The Open Theater, invited me to participate in their workshops, I began to recognize how belief can join politics to expand one's creativity. One series of meetings concerned Dante. In 1972, Chaikin asked Joseph Campbell and me to talk. The group wanted to know what gave the inferno its enduring human power. Campbell singled out archetypal Jungian patterns of guilt. I discussed Dante's theology of retribution. The shades in the circles of hell, I suggested, were punished by the sin itself. God gives back what we morally send out. In effect, the judgment of our life, I proposed, is our life. The group picked up on the dramatic potential of ultimate judgment alive in the present moment. Chaikin led the group in imagining a contemporary descent through hell that used bodily movements to trace a journey through inner reckoning. The experimental exercises based on the talks led to the 1972 performance of *Nightwalk* and a subsequent 1973 tour in Europe and at U.S. colleges. In New York during upheaving times I was finding people who were showing me new ways to grow as teacher and scholar while dealing with my need for faith.

On arrival my mind held a very personal map of New York: a maze of underground networks emitting pollution and noise with a big park bordered by silhouettes rising high from the bewilderment that sheltered museums, an opera house, and concert halls. I wanted its hum and buzz, clamor and all. With a friend's help I lucked out, finding a nondescript rent-controlled tenement flat on East 19th Street between First and Second avenues. The rent in 1967 was $98.00 for four railroad rooms and a slice-of-pound-cake bathroom. My bedroom looked out on what eventually became Stevie Wonder's 18th Street garden. In 1976, after drug addicts being treated at the nearby Beth Israel methadone center periodically burglarized my apartment, the city of fact broke through the city of desire.

Another friend guided me to a doorman building on Jane Street on the shabby-hip edge of Greenwich Village. The placed rocked. Men hit on one another in the elevator with "should we" or "shouldn't we" stares. New York gum-chewing humor murmured in the background. I immediately took to the neighborhood. Though on the outskirts, the area had a visible past and a lively street life, both high and low, that one couldn't miss. High-cheekbone WASPs eyed men wearing cornrows and tattoos. Much to my fascination, the area was on the move. Eventually the Whitney Museum would plan an annex on Gansevoort Street. Hotels were coming. A rotting elevated railroad line waited to be redesigned into the elegant High Line Park and promenade. Every aspect of the area was in the ascendancy, including the rents.

For all the newness, Old New York history was everywhere, in the district's foundation and outcroppings. There were Norway maple trees, Belgian cobblestones, and nineteenth-century townhouses, all emerging from Peter Stuyvesant's venerable farm to which the British had banished the popular Dutch governor. The Sanitation Department's garage on Gansevoort Street replaced a Customs House where Melville once worked. Jane Street ended at the Hudson River with the

Jane Street Hotel, a turn-of-the-century seamen's residence, where some survivors of the *Titanic* had been housed. One reportedly complained that her ship's cabin had been larger than her hotel room. There was room for everyone here. Cross-dressing prostitutes made themselves at home among the seedy alleys. Johns drove their Volvo station wagons with New Jersey license plates around with signs announcing "Baby on Board" in the rear window. With its history of accommodating survivors and outliers, the far West Village felt right for me.

These barebones facts of my immediate past brought Frank up to date about my current situation. The return east from northern Indiana had an emotional extension that he also needed to know because its geography would shape my movements in the future that I wished for us.

From East 19th Street near Gramercy Park and then from Jane Street in the Village, I took the New Jersey Transit bus 195 weekly to visit my mother and sister in Cedar Grove. We had dinner as a family and I skedaddled. That was it. Approximately forty miles back and forth marked the expanse of my terrain and the coordinating poles of my life.

In 1975, or thereabouts, my mother's arteries at seventy-five little by little hardened. Deprived of oxygen, her brain began to degenerate. The signs of physical and mental powers starting to fail were everywhere. Keys were lost. Mail vanished. So did her wedding ring. Her social brain was the first to give way. She didn't care. She didn't repeat herself because she spoke less and less. Gas remained lighted on the kitchen stove. Pots burned. My mother's appetite waned. Her mood flattened. She was traversing neural pathways with potholes. When the phone rang, she said hello without lifting up the receiver. She needed attention, and my sister loyally provided it. As is usually the case, the person in charge also needed help.

Marie would tough out caring for our mother to the point of being consumed by it. She was set in her filial Italian-American ways. Just as employing a cleaning person never occurred to my sister, hiring a stranger to care for our mother was unthinkable. The precedent for female self-donation was encoded in the family line. My mother and aunts cared for our grandmother, whose decline into dementia cast a long shadow over my mother and, in time, my sister as well. These female relatives seemed well loved as they got older—by their tight-knit female family within the family and most impressively by themselves. My mother and her sisters, Old World women, laid down the mantle of mother-caring that Marie picked up. She ably managed finances and the house.

I pitched in. Shopped for them at the Essex Green ShopRite, cooked, mopped up, and kept an eye on things. No sweat. Necessary tasks helped the day pass quickly when I was at their house. Inadvertently but surely, social visits turned into days of duty. Maybe by genetic link, a new place for me in their lives was taking hold. I was becoming mother to my mother and my sister's keeper. I'm not sure whether I was leading a double life of Village professor and suburban housekeeper or no life at all.

Because I never felt tightly bound by gender roles, crossing over to assume a traditionally female function came naturally and grew alongside my development as a man. The domestic chores were light and part-time, things I have always done for myself. Housework felt like the old errands I ran for the family as a boy. Helping my mother and sister evolved as an extension of the independent life I had embraced from the time I left for college at seventeen. Ever since living on my own as a graduate student, cooking was a pleasant ritual break from work at the desk. Housekeeping went with soul-keeping. It was not until an aunt, cousin, or visitor called attention to my visits that I picked up the transgressive implication for them of what I was doing. One relative said aloud to my sister that she couldn't count on her son's taking time out from his law practice to help her if she ever needed the help.

Though gender equality brought about by feminism was very much in the air, and though gender fluidity was integral to my personal and academic life, a man doing women's work called attention to himself in suburban New Jersey. In that conventional environment, particularly that of Italian Americans, everyday routines of domesticity and caring were and remain the norm for women. Traditional expectation exerted greater pressure on my family in which middle-class assumptions of female responsibility were reinforced by Italian immigrant mores. Expediency cleared the way for my mother and sister to overcome their gender rigidities. Because I was male, family tradition set the bar of household affairs low for me. Even so, I was breaking the rules. Other norms hovered to be breached as further borders had to be passed on my mothering journey. Those offenses against sexism were part of the appeal.

These were the days when I started to call my mother Nellie, the familial American substitute for Nicolina, with which she was baptized in Italy in January 1900. The younger my mother got in old age, the more her real name Nellie suited her. When I arrived through the front door or garage, I called out, "Hi, Nell!" The greeting was meant to cheer her by announcing a companion's arrival. The gesture achieved it goal.

Using the personal names Nell or Nellie felt right for the feelings evolving between us. Amicability unfettered the apron strings to free us both to be the new selves arising from my maternal concern for my mother's dependency. At this point, I no longer had to dismantle the power of the idealized mother. In truth, I never really knew her as mother. Does anyone know her or his mother as mother? Calling her Nellie marked a new and truer way of knowing her. Nellie responded warmly to being called Nell. Previously, I properly called her Mother (never the informal Mom or Ma). Like Nellie, I welcomed the playfulness that attended our reversing relationship.

The world of motherly providence held no end of conflict and exposure—a revelation. I tried to fool myself into thinking that bygones were bygones. Past disagreements did modulate into forgiveness, but mercy inflicted the wounds of love. The steady work of caring for an old woman cut a channel of intimacy that threatened. The closer we got, the more the breakdown of Nellie's mind and body, like a herald of definitive self-reckoning, called me back to myself. Nellie could pierce the soul to bare what was in the heart.

Happily, no force field shielded me from the cumulative influence of Nellie's love. In a word, Nellie was a woman who gave herself to others and loyally nurtured her nerdy son. She treated me as her only child, without ever warning me that the world would deal with me as one of many. The kind, unobtrusive habit of her being was there all along in gifts of blood and spirit that later came to term in the sustenance set at the Lord's Table. Now, from the position of what I have become I'll try to capture through a few luminous moments of her early life how Nellie was.

Nicolina Cordileone was born January 15, 1900, in Campochiaro, the tiny hilltop pre-Roman settlement inside the Matese mountains of Abruzzi where her mother and father were born (of that bleak origin, more later). At five Nicolina joined the mass departure of Italian peasants who crossed the Atlantic in rickety ships to the United States. If foreign-born, Nellie was American-bred. She simply replanted her roots in America. Resettlement gave her as much of a home as she would ever have, one that for Nellie was invariably provisional. Her mother was an orphan and left Nellie with an uncertain sense of belonging. Nellie seemed always to be testing the cultural waters as much for danger as for rightful context. She conveyed a sense of being homesick for a world elsewhere, longing for a place that anchored her soul.

Nellie's inner nature came through in her earliest recollection of childhood. It concerned an episode on the *Madonna*, an aptly named ship that brought her here. The raw winter sea of late November 1905 kicked up a horrifying storm. Grandma was shaken and naturally worried about her two young daughters, seven and five. She ordered the girls to remain in steerage with the other immigrants. The older daughter, Tessie, obeyed, but a stronger command ruled the younger Nellie.

To a mountain girl, the cattle-class pen had to be entrapping next to an unfettered storm. In her mature retelling, my mother seemed to utter the excited child's desire: Let the drenching wind come! She would have it, and she did. Perhaps the girl could also prove her nerve to her fearful mother. Whatever the motive, Nellie darted out from the dankness below to run around the pitching main deck and give her body up to the waves. It was all play and freedom. Nellie returned indoors elated. Grandma, terrified by her child's absence, slapped Nellie's face for being disobedient. The whack knocked off an earring pierced in Nellie's ear. A child's endangering herself certainly justified discipline; but because running out into the storm was Nellie's reaching out for joy on her own, the reprimand was felt to be irrational, unfair. Headstrong at five, Nellie was soul-struck at sea.

Grandma's blow struck at the root of Nellie's nature, her dignity. The lesion never healed. Nor did she stop telling the story. Whenever she did, her chin tilted upward like that of a boxer who had taken a clout. She inhabited the pain because defiance brought back the psychological prize of liberty gained at sea. I can still hear her voice strong enough for the world to hear saying that she would take on enemies of her personal freedom. Nellie's life was forged in deliberate response to restriction. Her inner determination won my young admiration.

Nellie's private will shaped her body. She never again wore an earring. She never wore jewelry. Her face was bare of makeup. In her eighty-six years Nellie used neither cologne nor deodorant. She would scrub her body as if to rub off weakness. Her hair was brushed back into a tight bun. Her frame was trim. Austerity checked her tongue. She preferred smiling or frowning to speaking.

After the earring, there was the fabric. She was fourteen, in the second year at the Newark girls' vocational high school, learning how to sew. Nellie was so neat-fingered that the teacher invited her to work with advanced students on an end-of-term project. That was a big deal. Each girl could design and make her own dress. Nellie was in her glory with the creative privilege to make something on her own. Every detail of the assignment brought delight. The students had to buy their own fabric. Choosing the right material for her design made her feel self-sufficient. In the yard goods section in the bargain basement of Bamberger's department store, Nellie found just the green floral cotton print for her sketch. Relentlessly sensible, she made sure we knew that her pattern was serviceable, not frilly. The fabric required for the dress came to 25 cents. I have no idea what a quarter in 1914 is now worth; but the price was too steep for Grandma, who always reacted as the destitute orphan worried about a rainy day. She refused to give Nellie the quarter.

Nellie told the story many times. Whenever she reached the point of Grandma's refusal, Nellie's voice tightened, and I visualized a bird being shot down just as it was about to take flight in early morning.

But the fledgling seamstress would be on the wing again. She shed not a tear, said not a word. She quit vocational school. Pride cost, and she would pay its price, however dear. Thereafter she kept herself to herself. Within her there rested inherited mountain grit that empowered her for the life ahead.

In her mature years, Nellie's reserve put her in the shadow of female Italian neighbors, who favored an Anna Magnani sensuality and solidarity. The usual assumptions about Italian women did not apply to Nellie. Rather than stand out, she stood apart, with grace and forethought. The courtesy she showed others came back to her. People respected Nellie. No one outside the family called my mother by her first name or Nellie or Nell. With a bit of *soggezione*—to use the term for respect tinged with awe—lingering from the old Italian customs, everyone in our little corner of southwest Newark addressed her as Mrs. Giannone, occasionally as *signora*. That our family owned rental property in the area added to the deference shown Nellie. If as a child I wanted my mother to be more like other mothers so that I could feel more like their boys, her decorous bearing nevertheless added to my affection for her. Love, she showed me, originated in dignity. Her bending of social forms went hand-in-glove with the way her independence made it okay to be dissimilar from others. Nellie gave me permission to be different. This was another gift for a lifetime.

Being different actually came with being Giannone. My father, Salvatore, a burly, outgoing man, also occupied a valued place of his own. The moment in 1912 that he set foot on Ellis Island, he was raring to go. A determined sixteen-year-old, he had the work ethic of a beaver that embraced a clannish loyalty minted in Italian mountains. He was a foreman for a succession of asphalt paving companies and so had the power to hire local Italian men as day laborers. From steady earnings, he bought several buildings in our blue-collar Newark neighborhood in the 1930s. One of his jobs was being in charge of surfacing the roads for the 1939–40 New York World's Fair in Queens. I knew my father counted, because the family got free passes for the exhibitions and rides. The Russians gave him a kilo of caviar for repairing the drainage ditch around their building. The unfamiliar delicacy was lost on my parents and the neighbors who got small Mason jars full of the shiny black globules.

Our family's advantage during the Depression discomfited Nellie. Tenants coming personally every month to pay their rent in cash brought their personal hardship too close to her. Owing or being owed something involved matters of self-respect and its possible loss. When the woman upstairs from us could not pay her rent after her husband injured himself at work, my mother said nothing and probably came off as insensitive to the troubled family, when in actuality Nellie over-identified with those experiencing shame. To be witness to or cause of such exposure reopened her remembered trauma of shame.

Nellie had a gift for reading the heart. A woman known to my mother only by her abject poverty brought not tears to Nellie but a call for silent action. Packing serviceable children's clothes in paper bags, Nellie from time to time walked two blocks to the back stairs of the tenement where the woman's family lived and left the garments at the back door of the family's flat on the top floor. She trod lightly along mean streets and left no traces of her goodwill. She had no stomach for attention. Once, when I was four or five, I tagged along as she discreetly deposited the clothes. Ever since then I have held anonymous decency in high regard.

Her sensitivity to privation and suffering made Nellie acutely sensitive to violence. Aggression of course pervaded immigrant Newark life. The Italian code of virility added honor to cruelty. Hostile body language set in during boyhood and lasted through late middle age. With the bully as local avatar of manliness, physical violence was real and a daily occurrence. It was not uncommon for boys to have rock fights, aiming to hit the head. It was children reenacting the military wars around us that Nellie could not bear. She once covered her face with her hands to check the impulse to scream aloud when seeing children in a free-for-all inflicting pain on one another. She did not lose her cool. But I nearly do now while envisioning her palpable hurt.

She tried and largely failed to tamp down my youthful aggression. I didn't always back down from fights. I did enjoy sharing in military games with friends and bigoted cowboys-and-Indians brawls while aware that Nellie disapproved of them. My verbal combativeness probably compensated for her instructing me not to strike back physically in retribution. While World War II raged, she forbade my wearing the combat fatigues that boys sported. A model tank, bayonet, and gun (my trusty slingshot, too) were outright forbidden in the house. She despised war. The unbridled patriotism that exulted in killing horrified Nellie. During hot and cold wars, such political views were anomalous in a gung ho neighborhood of naturalized citizens. Free of ideology, her opposition to violence and war prepared the way for my pacifist commitment in later years. Once again, Nellie's influence won out in the long run.

Nellie's inconspicuous ways were noticeable in her children's schooling. She fervently encouraged her children to get the education she had forfeited. The hardheaded, impulsive teenage dropout became a patient teacher in her thirties. Before I went to kindergarten, she taught me to read. Her method was homespun. When she saw me pointing to words out of curiosity in the *Newark Star-Ledger*, she seized my interest, pronounced the words, and gave their meaning. I was to repeat each word and explain what it meant. After I put several words together, Nellie insisted that that I remove my hand from the newspaper because finger-reading would hamper my understanding the full sentence.

Nellie advanced with me through grammar school. She got the readings for the next fall and bought the books for summer reading. She was frugal about expenses, but never with buying books. On books I could splurge. I did and still do. Year after year, for thirty minutes a day, Nellie and I sat at the kitchen table with the textbooks. I read aloud and fast—as I sped through practicing piano—so I could get to the crafts table at West Side Park. Nellie slowed me down to correct mistakes. In the fifth grade my haste earned me a C for sloppy penmanship. The following summer, after thirty minutes of reading, I had to spend another thirty minutes undoing my abrupt upright lines in favor of the ladylike purling script of the Palmer method. The best I did in the sixth grade was a B in penmanship. It was for Nellie a blotch on my report card that she let slide.

Nothing else about school escaped Nellie's attention. She prevented my being a patrol boy directing students across streets because being one would expose me to bad weather. She did approve my editing the school paper—writing took place indoors and dealt with words. When the teachers wanted me to skip the first half of the sixth grade, however, Nellie put her foot down. With two years of high school behind her, a self-possessed, elfin Italian housewife with masculine power and possessed of a certain refinement marched into the principal's office and told him that skipping one term would break the September–June academic cycle and interfere with the traditional high school and college academic year. I finished the full eight years in sequence. As for college, which was outside the neighborhood radar screen, that was a foregone conclusion for Nellie.

When I finished elementary school, Nellie graduated to the next level of mentoring. She did not want me to attend Webster Junior High School followed by West Side High School in Newark. They offered a poor education in what she called a "roughneck" environment. From my schoolteacher Aunt Rose, Nellie heard about St. Benedict's Prep, run by monks in downtown Newark, and the diocesan Seton Hall Prep in suburban South Orange. Both were Catholic boys' schools, but religion and gender were irrelevant. Quality of education alone mattered to Nellie.

My father had misgivings about a private school. His concern was not the cost. With money he was generous, with competitive class feelings less so. Although few children attended the local Catholic grammar school, no child in the family or immigrant neighborhood went to a costly private high school. Such an exception for me would make me stick out—as though being gay at thirteen I didn't already—and might encourage me to think that I was better than the family and others. Difference and advantage were fine with Nellie. She prevailed. I chose Seton Hall Prep's grass over St. Benedict's concrete.

The curriculum was classical. Latin was mandatory for the first two years. Nellie was curiously in awe of her son's studying this venerable language. Something noble and cultural entered her home and life. Under the guise of helping me, she could participate in the learned world of her desire. And so every weekday evening after supper at the kitchen table, Nellie checked the vocabulary list that ended each daily Latin lesson. She gave me the English word, and I was to give the Latin equivalent. "Boy," she drilled; "*Puer,*" I answered. Then she repeated "*puer,*" and I impatiently threw back "boy." She saw me through two years of declensions and conjugations and habitually sprang surprise quizzes, "OK, now spell it." "*A-m-o, a-m-a-s, a-m-a-t.*" Ostensibly, Nellie was testing me, but I knew that she was veiling her inability to pronounce the Latin words properly. Nellie earned a good grade in Latin each of the four semesters. She did well in French too.

When I got to geometry, biology, and physics, the kitchen tutorials ended; but Nellie was always behind me with encouragement. Nellie knew when to intervene and, more influentially, when to smile and let go. Instinctive wisdom about considering others was another dimension of her moral style. That was the case when I fell in love with opera at a young age. Because Nellie encouraged my listening to the Saturday matinee Metropolitan Opera broadcasts, I didn't feel self-conscious being the only kid enthralled with high Cs and cabalettas. Actually, I believed the other boys were missing out on something marvelous.

After high school, Nellie and I were on our own to educate ourselves. Though I pulled away, far away, she never broke with me. She basked in the reflected achievement of my studies even if that meant I chose a profession in which she held no place. It made her happy that I was doing what I longed to do. When the blood supply to Nellie's brain began to slow down in the early 1970s, we were together again. Then I became a student at the kitchen table and her bedside. This time Nellie schooled me in the curriculum of affliction. A dear woman, a fine parent. My involvement with her sickness and dying extended and fulfilled her devotion to me. Before such power of loyalty I stand beholden.

When I told Frank about my ties with my mother, I was factual to the point of perhaps seeming emotionally withholding about the place he recently occupied in my life. Describing my New Jersey responsibilities could have suggested that there was little room for him, which was not by any means how I felt. After all, it was Frank who was teaching me that by giving my heart to one I could give my heart to others. My affection for him was more than a fling from aloneness, though that escape steered my passion. I did not say *love*, but love for him was in me. What I felt was a possibility, an emotion on which to build a future.

Years of fear, however, edited exuberance out of all my emotions, both in experiencing and communicating them. After initial caution, nonetheless, Frank was unwary. He had poured out his heart. In doing so, he revealed a talent for giving back my self in a tender form that was brought into being by his open affection. He saw me as better and more ready for a committed life than I was. In reality, I was raised not for love as a mutually enriching involvement but for a love of obligation. I knew early on that if there were days and years to come between Frank and me, I would have to rise to the occasion of his moral imagination. I did try to reflect how he saw me when he moved in with me in March 1982. Living together was his idea that soon became my physical and moral necessity.

Frank's trust in his feelings taught me basic lessons about the spiritual doctrine of friendship that the Catholic church had neglected to impart to me. This knowledge was in Frank's bones. With him, love was not gendered, any more than heroism and holiness were confined to male and female domains. Nor was there danger of a Manichean or Gnostic rejection of sexual life in favor of spiritual life. The affair of the libido had the power to be the affair of one's entire being. Love directed toward another person was for Frank love directed toward God.

Frank's understanding of human bonds called to mind Augustine's celebrating male companions as vital to his conversion. Augustine is blunt about our being wired for profound attachment: Our nature overwhelmingly desires "to love and be loved." The longing arises from the way God designed things. Creation, in Augustine's moral economy, impresses on the human heart the tendency toward friendship into which God has also built a need for physical expression of the love that friendship can bring into being. "A friend," Augustine avows, "is one with whom one may dare to share the counsels of one's heart." Notably receptive to the affection of others, the *servi Dei*, the servants of God, the austere, erudite, and expansive Augustine, seemed never to be alone.

I took the plunge with Frank. Our relationship—more precisely, the hard work of our love—supported an evolution of the heart. Frank's counsel to me to remain vulnerable—accompanied by his significant silences—made more meaningful my friendship with my mother and sister, two women he had yet to meet but had already helped. He was showing me how to make room for others in my life. To be sure, we were alone, but being alone together was a bond against isolation that felt like a point of entry to ultimate matters.

My journey to these women was long, and the path was filled with barriers. Wanting to be truly alive to my sexuality got in the way of my being with my family. I could handle being gay and tried to manage their presumed disapproval. And so I developed the time-tested strategy of concealment that I learned early and well as a gay kid when exposure of an aberrant sexuality meant ridicule from other boys, denunciation by society, disgrace for the family, and condemnation from the Catholic church. My being gay could hurt them. It hurt me only if it hurt them.

At every turn, I had to defend myself. To overcome the threats in advance, I got good grades in school to gain affirmation in myself and from teachers and family. I developed verbal skills to parry the expected insults to my dignity. Being like other males and achieving merely what they did was not enough. After all, homosexuality made me different, an incomplete male. Males tested my sense of worth. I had to do better than other males in order to be their equal. These tactics worked to get me through decades of projected hostility lurking in reality. The success I attained exacted a price. I came to believe that aloneness was my nature as a gay person.

The culture and the church may have begun the process of exclusion, but I cooperated in setting myself apart. I understood my immigrant family's detachment from homosexuality and shielded them from my different nature. Without support from my family or the church or the moral atmosphere to resist the ruling denigration, I inevitably internalized cultural rejection. At the same time that I took on the judgment, I believed that the social and religious authorities were wrong and unjust. I found the New Jersey prerequisites for masculinity to repress feelings and elevate violence. Early on I tried to rise above the code by feeling superior, and I have ever since been (not unwisely, it turns out) hostile toward established forms of authority. Like Dante throwing sop to pass the monster Cerberus in the inferno, I fed society what it battened on to get by ogres guarding the entrance to social acceptance.

A more sober feeling counterbalanced my immature conceit. At the center of my young inner world was a conviction that though by social lights my attraction to men violated divine and human law, my sexual desire was also a part of a transcendent life. This healthier sense of myself came to my unformed consciousness as naturally as did oxygen to my lungs. Only later did I find out that believing homosexuality shared in holiness was sacrilegious. Still later, much later, did I realize that such blasphemy was actually on to a truth of my sexuality's share in an inviolable life. I have since held fast to the belief that gay men and lesbians live under providence and that we were fully and completely created in the image and likeness of the divine.

Against the power systems of church and state, I believed in the rightness of homosexuality. This trust came not from Catholic instruction about individual dignity but from my fundamental perception of the world as divinely planned and therefore supportive of human aspirations to be fully alive. Even when feeling estranged from things, as I consistently have been, the world felt coherent and therefore held a place for me as a gay man to seek the source of life.

My inchoate trust may have been irreverent, but I had just enough hope to keep looking for the gay person's share in the divine scheme. Emotionally, this bedrock spiritual confidence spared me from anger. To be sure, many gay men found their rightful place through the political use of fury. Stonewall hastened everyone's coming of age. Angry men confronted the raw assertion of police power during one of the cops' routine raids on gay bars. Gay people would no longer conform to what straight fantasy said about them as passive and criminal. They would not be pushed around by their sexuality.

Welcome to the Greenwich Village of the outraged and outrageous. Here in the middle of sleepy all-night smoke shops and grocery stores, defiance ignited open rebellion. How's this for a curtain-raiser to the main production? Faggots turned the tables to fuel the fire against their torturers. At first, the bartender and some irate patrons of the Stonewall Inn fought back. Their boldness inspired others. In the dark early morning hours of late June 1969, the smoldering gay revolution erupted. The next night, others joined the fight against police harassment. Young, racy go-go dancers got off the stage and hit the rowdy streets to help open the drama of blatant espousals of sexual freedom. It was nothing short of amazing to see what insurgency looked like in New York City at mid-twentieth century. This uprising was life-giving. Because I can think of no other gay victory to celebrate, the holiday of Stonewall remains a favorite—a festival of unmasking that put the culture on trial and opened the way for self-reclamation.

Transvestites, for whom politics was always theatrical, assumed starring roles. (Cross-dressing was a crime in 1969.) With a magnificent bravura all their own, the drag queens threw punches at the cops one minute and twirled around the next minute to blow kisses to the admiring mob assembled in Sheridan Square that shouted back, "Go, girl, go!" Nonexistent in society defined by male power, androgynous persons were revolutionary stars on the political stage. The protesters' roar and gestures carried in their tumult the display of communal sexual woundedness. To be aggressively in the thick of insurgence had to be elating. The very stones of the Village streets seemed to cry out in rejoicing support. The full-throated message went out to the world. Flaming to the highest power of camp, gay people brought their mocked pretentious gesticulations to a peak of historic influence. The impact resounds even now through every avant-garde gallery, gay pride parade, state legislature, academic discipline, and medical practice. The resolve to set gay life free has been sustained by the determination to live it out.

One more point about gay activism, and then I'll drop the subject, for now. The aims of the movement's hard left made life freer for me. It is also true, and no credit to me, that I drifted along the political sidelines. Italian to the core, I nevertheless put five fingers to my mouth, kissed them, waved them, and saluted, *"Bravissimi!"* My ingrained habit for self-protection was to say something without saying it.

I would not set my heart on anything the loss of which would break it. Even though one never shows anyone anything, I would show the world—as Nellie tried—that I needed neither its acceptance nor its support. The upshot was not true freedom but a madcap declaration of the very need for the human connections I denied. My discounting traditional relations evolved into a delusion of autonomy anchored in a subtle pride. This pride had its own hubris, its own deep loneliness.

4   School for Trust

You will have found Christ when you are concerned with other
people's suffering and not your own.

—Flannery O'Connor, *The Habit of Being*

The Christmas holidays were the right time for introductions. I had a
new relation prepared for my mother and sister as a present. With a
certain suppressed exhilaration, I invited Frank for an early Saturday
dinner to meet Nellie and Marie at their home in Cedar Grove. They
knew only that a friend was coming to join us.

No bell-bottom trousers over western boots this time. Frank wore a
blue sweater, gray flannel trousers, and loafers, his Sunday best, a mantle of praise, as Isaiah says a guest should put on. Homage also shone
through his morning-sun smile and two dozen pink tea roses that were
outsized enough nearly to hide his 5′5″ stature. The extravagance of
Frank's thoughtfulness (he was flat broke) was the hallmark of his
nature. His innate modesty of putting generosity ahead of anything
personal he might bring won Marie over instantly. When Marie was
relaxed, Nellie smiled. Frank had a familiarity with people that revealed the inner man of the cloth in him. Strangers were at their ease
with him. I found that sexy. He had a genius for making friends.

By the winter of 1981, numerous ischemic attacks had ransacked
Nellie's brain and left amyloidal plaques in their wake, but I did not
have to account for Nellie's mental condition to Frank. He understood innocence and emotional poverty. Unafraid of tenderness,
Frank wanted in advance to love the older women I loved. There was

nothing in it for him. Open affection was second nature. His self-giving was a like a pebble dropped in water. It sent encompassing ripples out to Nellie, whose afflictions from mental disease were on full display. Eighty-one years old, pale, and wizened with stringy salt white hair, Nellie weighed no more than 100 pounds. She wore one of her many buttoned shirts with open collar, this time tan, and dark brown pants. Nothing fancy. Decorations never suited her. Nor did small talk, ever. Nellie's soul was truly a creature of silence. The day Frank visited, Nellie sat patiently in a beige upholstered living room chair that had an absorbent pad to cover the urine stains she left in the pillow, smudges that got bigger with washing. As one among others, Nellie was the source and recipient of soft feelings. Her porous presence united us, so that we could fleetingly be one through sacred ties without her occupying the center of attention.

The ease of being together was the wonder of it all. Nothing was forced. For a number of years Nellie's mental incapacity created a setting in which emotions and things were rendered rather than stated. In the moment of meeting, Nellie's trust greeted Frank. Behind Nellie's clear, lightly shaded green eyes was a direct engagement with the situation involving a stranger. Her peaceful body told us that. Thanks to the well-being Marie provided for Nellie, the secure familiar absorbed the new visitor. The moment was full enough for Nellie.

Nellie had a rightful place of her own just as she was. Her reason and voice were gone; her body was worn, to be sure, like her face scored by sustained pen-strokes of time, and there was not much physical presence left in her. But there was another kind of presence: a forbearing acceptance of the losses besetting her. Life on reduced, dependent terms seemed to satisfy her. True, Nellie's typical mothering days were far behind her. Yet in letting them calmly slip away, she was parenting us in how to accept what we cannot avoid. Nearly twenty-five years earlier, I felt the same mothering in my dying grandmother and have identified this final surrender with old women. They were lessons in learning and forgetting and learning anew.

She who lived in shadows, more than those who lived in the full light of day, showed me the lines laid out for me in aging, lines that also led back to the inner dark of my sister, mother, and mother's mother. Here Frank and I were with a confounding future before us. There were many patterns for constructing my life of sexual adventure with Frank, but there was no blueprint for how two men build romance on caring for an old woman who was losing her mind.

Frank's meeting aged Nellie brought back my boyhood visits to my maternal grandmother. Grandma was unlike anyone else around the Italian neighborhood in Newark. That rarity and her utter plainness captivated me. Though from peasant stock, she bore the patrician name Maria Teresa Castelli Cordileone. For years Grandma suffered the mental deterioration that subsequently afflicted my mother and touched my sister. Frequently after school, I walked three blocks from our house in Newark on the top of Fifteenth Avenue and South 15th Street down the hill three short blocks to Grandma's home on South 12th Street.

Grandma, like my father's family, came from the tiny rough-hewn town of Campochiaro, which hovers high in the Abruzzo Mountains in the Molise region. I descend from tribal intermarriage. Inbreeding and the recent scientific findings linking the maternal line with susceptibility to Alzheimer's make me wonder if my boyhood path to Grandma charted my neurological destination. Both the Cordileone and Giannone sides of my family issued from problematic Italian obscurity.

I visited Campochiaro in December 1960 during a Fulbright year in Italy. Getting to the spot took some doing. From Rome one took the slow train eastbound to Campobasso, the provincial capital, and got off midway at Boiano and hiked or, if lucky, found a taxi to ride about ten steep miles upward to the crest that is Campochiaro. The church occupied the pinnacle and with its noble spire towered over the town and valley below. Alongside the church, a tablet honored those killed in World War I. The people spoke only the local vernacular, which mashed dialects from nearby regions with Greek and Albanian. The lingo was nearly as incomprehensible as was the speakers' communal isolation. Surviving in that barrenness took immense effort and exacted great suffering. Until after World War II, Abruzzo had sheepherders, dirt-poor tenant farmers, prehistoric boulders, earthquakes, and an overmastering clergy. That was it.

Campochiaro, as its name boasts, occupies a lofty field with clear views—breathtaking sights—of the surrounding Matese Mountains and valleys. Like other isolated villages in Abruzzo, Campochiaro sees itself as its own *paese*, or country, with its own language and customs. Daily living in the town was the hardscrabble province writ lower, smaller, and poorer than I imagined. Food and shelter were skimpy. Sheep outnumbered humans and had an easier time existing than did people. Around 1900, when my father was a boy, it was a fiefdom. Political power then was in the fisted, grasping hands of the local priest, upon whose memory my father never missed the chance to heap in dialect Italian the same torrent of curses. To escape the cruelty of the life they inherited, many left at the turn of the twentieth century for a better, freer life in America. That universal desire brought my father and his four brothers here.

Although scattered, *paesani* never forgot their roots because the town's cut-off rural life forged a bond to the local dirt and rocks that was firmer than ties to nationality. That attachment was not mine. I left Campochiaro with a clear-eyed realization that the path homeward led to another separation. Besides a time-lag, there was a cultural gap. Life as a contemporary gay American removed me from my family's primitive birthplace, the cliff's edge where my father's fathers and my mother's mothers were buried. These colossal mountains too melt like wax before the Lord. I never returned to the desolate Abruzzo highlands.

Grandma was the link to Campochiaro. I doubt that Grandma suffered the trauma of dislocation because emotionally she never left the rocky ledge where she was born. Grandpa, however, took to American possibilities. He worked for both the Pennsylvania Railroad and the Delaware and Lackawanna Railroad. With a poor man's eye for security, he cannily bought property he could rent out to recent immigrants. Grandma only looked back to Abruzzo. Its hardships were all that the old woman knew and all she seemed to need, except for the filial devotion of her six daughters, four of whom lived long enough to care for their unassimilated mother to her death in exotic America.

Grandma was a notable exception to the driving force that was changing the United States and her family. Europeans sought a fresh start in the strange land. Not Grandma. She brought her entire biography, with its old heart, old vision, and old love, to new America.

Grandma landed in America from Naples on the *Madonna* on November 15, 1905, with her two oldest daughters, Aunt Tessie and my mother, Nellie. Grandma put her stoical imprint on the journey. Because Grandpa felt that his wife and two small girls needed comfort and privacy during the long crossing, he sent Grandma enough money for first-class accommodations, which on this hulking transport were by no means luxurious or commodious. The expensive booking also meant they could avoid the ordeal of Customs and immediately disembark to meet Grandpa, who would be at Ellis Island to meet them. Habituated as Grandma was to adversity, she regarded such an expense for personal benefit as wasteful; and so she cashed in the tickets for steerage space to save money. As a result, mother and two girls ended up being processed on Ellis Island for two days, bewildered Grandpa waiting for them on the pier.

The three Cordileone females did make it here safely if battered during the voyage. They rode the crest of first-wave Italian migrants. Grandma, however, was caught in an undertow. From the time this displaced *contadina* settled in Jersey City and then moved to Newark, she rarely ventured outside her house. Though family and Italian immigrants surrounded Grandma, she was ethnically and personally if not legally segregated in America. Cultural anxiety held her hostage. Forever poor, forever rootless, she made herself a shut-in long before age and dementia confined her.

To me Grandma was the craggy, outlandish place called Italy in stark human form. Rejection shrouded both woman and her native land. Her foreignness flowed into me and stayed like a murmur in my blood, distant and silent, but always inside me. Her isolation seized me and worked its way into the estrangement I felt in being gay. Just like me, Grandma was full of fears and secrets.

Grandma at all times wore the garb of domestic privacy. Except for attending Mass at St. Rocco Church with her daughters for certain feasts days (St. Lucy's Day was one) she deemed necessary to celebrate, she wore what my aunts called a housedress. A simple short-sleeved cotton garment with buttons down the front, usually light blue with small white flower prints or white with small blue floral patterns, loosely wrapped her wide-hipped, small, bony frame. Her haggard face was calm; her body had no breasts. When I arrived at Grandma's home, the reclusive old woman had only to shuffle along in her worn slippers out of her bedroom into the kitchen to catch my heart. She clearly enjoyed being herself, aging and all. As far as I could tell, she didn't seek approval from others. Nor was she judgmental toward others.

Grandma's footsore and weary appearance had a potent immediacy. An avatar in ripe old age of a broken, uneducated past, she was the first person I knew who made me wonder how she made her way through the day in a totally unfamiliar world. To a gay kid without a context her staying power was reassuring and captivating. Sadness was part of the hook. As was her vulnerable aloneness. Without her teeth—both upper and lower dentures were kept in a glass of water by the kitchen sink—her face looked caved in. The only fullness of her head came from her gray hair, usually combed back into a bun. Her light-brown eyes, though, had kindness. Grandma shambled along just thinking whatever she thought, just feeling whatever she felt, in the same way that she sleepwalked into and through America for more than fifty years. The old woman haunted me. Was that all there was to being a grownup? Did advanced age mean removal from the excitement of the social world? Would I too get to the point of dragging my feet? Would I be quietly amenable when a nosy little boy came to visit me?

My confusion was another part of the astonishment. Grandma seemed to experience seclusion with ease and made a day and a life out of it, with the help of homemade wine and a patron saint. On the bedroom dresser was a foot-high statue with a chipped hand and draped in a light-blue robe and green rosary beads of Grandma's namesake, St. Teresa—which Teresa didn't matter—set on a plain white dish that held pennies, nickels, and dimes. Were the coins there for convenience or as votive offering? Was Grandma religious?

From her devotions, I assumed that Jesus was Italian and had come over on the boat from the other side with Grandma. Did religion have anything to do with God? Did Grandma have God's attention and therefore didn't need to learn English or to be noticed by the world? Had Grandma become a friend of death? How does time pass for her without piano lessons, books, and homework? She seemed satisfied with a restricted life, biding her time to fill the vacuum left by immigration. That amazed a young, impatient boy whose life was so exultantly ahead of him.

Our visit followed a slow ritual set by the boundaries of Grandma's generosity. Grandma and I sat alone in maple chairs at her kitchen table with blue enamel top for about twenty minutes. Without asking if I wanted anything to eat, she usually went to the gas stove where cannellini beans seemed always soaking; dipped dried, crusty pieces of bread in the murky bean water; put the spongy hunks in a white ceramic soup bowl; and sprinkled the drenched mounds with green olive oil and coarse salt. Eating the pungent bread gave me the feeling that I was doing something good for Grandma and myself. When I lived at the American Academy in Rome in 1983, I found and bought four plain Genori bowls identical to Grandma's at a rundown Trastevere *bottega*.

Of Grandma's familiar company I never tired even though she hardly spoke and barely changed expression. Sometimes she sat motionless like a bust or portrait in a museum. She looked at or past me, just as I looked at her. Fresh feelings came and I took more pleasure in recognizing her usual tranquil and composed appearance than in seeking a new one. A backward glance affords a portal in our visits. The full effect of her presence depended on the late sun's settling on the scene from the kitchen window. In that resplendent domestic light Grandma presiding over the table with a dish of sodden bread shone unforgettably like a woman in a Vermeer niche piece. In 1960 when I lived in Trieste I learned that the soup plate held *pane cotto*, a staple of *cucina povera*, and that Grandma's treat was a poor person's fare too humble even for a lowdown *trattoria* to serve. Oh yes, Grandma gave me a coin from St. Teresa's plate when I left her kitchen to go home. Although Grandma had ten grandchildren, her quiet welcome and gentle doting made me feel special among many. But in truth, she was a mystery. I could tell how she felt only by her simple hospitality and my gratitude.

This is not a melancholy tale of a sweet old Italian lady, her offspring, and sister immigrants. Their courtesy and traditional life were only a covering. They had their rough sides and inwardly were as hard as nails. The aging female heart can seem strange. Little about their obvious defects could be mistaken for charm, which at best is elusive. Like the aged young men with AIDS toddling around Chelsea in the 1980s, many old women struck the popular onlooker in the Newark of my 1930s childhood as showing us what to fear—namely, decay, insignificance, and death.

The old women who wore widows' black from head to foot were a perturbing and claustral sight. Phantoms from meager ways of life, ghosts from another era, they signaled backwardness and cultural clash to children of Italian immigrants who wanted to hurtle their way into modern American ways. Aged women embarrassed people. The listless amble of these bent, dim figures carried around a permanent state of mourning that initially struck me when a small boy as drab, inhospitable.

Grandma's aura gave these silhouettes of bereavement a prescient place in my heart. Long before living close to death made spiritual sense to me, aging females embodied my origin and destiny. Theirs was not their story alone. It was also mine. They became custodians of a slow-motion drama involving the aspirations of lost *paesani* from long-relinquished tribal settlements in the high deserts of the Abruzzo and Calabria mountains.

Everybody has a little bit of the old woman in them. In my case, a lot of her talent shapes my longing to attain the fullness of life in matters of daily living and human relationships. The old woman embodies a fortunate condition of the spirit forged in the crucible approaching death. Such skill has many faces. In ancient patristic writing, a male who is mature in years and wisdom and whose advice is sought is a *geron*, the Greek word for old man. The word *geraia* carries the same honor for such a seasoned old woman. Classical Greek, however, invokes far too much learning and refinement to describe the elderly females in my life. The colloquial Italian *vecchia* strikes the right note of commonness and gritty bodily struggle. Their good judgment came not in fine speech or considered reflection on the world. Speculation that motivated was beyond them. These women strengthened rather than inspired. And they could be exasperating. Their rhythms and sonorities clung to a course of conduct that seemed outworn. To know them one had to know them well, and I wanted to. It was good to be close to old women. These ripened females bore spiritual gifts in what they did not say and how they lived their sickness and dying. Each followed a path congenial to her soul. Whether she had faith in God or not, she seemed to fulfill herself under the spirit. Her very being was a quality of knowing that abutted my deep heart.

The *vecchia*'s knowing reaches into lonely places I have needed to know about. She gestures to a place where ego is incidental. And yet, her will to live remains unbroken. She puts up no defense against the claims of death. Facing death renews her. She takes no refuge in the expectation of heavenly reward. Lacking a known future, she is tranquil. The present suffices. Lacking physical agility, she advances inward. The ways in which her spirit moves while she sits motionless hint of guidance about living amid desolation. She removes herself cautiously, a moving away from discord to be free of care so that she is free to love. She abides without pomp. Going unnoticed satisfies her. She still feels affection for people and places, but love comes through less as an emotion than as a habit of her distilled being. The old crone's love of life at life's end touches me as a motion of the mind, whether intact, broken, or mended. Ripeness is the basis from which the *vecchia*'s identity unfolds.

Often I think of myself as growing beyond gender into androgyny. Especially when making an allowance for my last years in a world that is not my own, I feel that I can do no better than to have the unsentimental disposition of an old woman. Hope has a dry, flattened chest and wears a wrinkled face with gray-white hair.

This encomium to the *vecchia* no doubt came from projections of qualities that made up for my deficiencies. Truth be told, loneliness and grief may not have made these old women wise. What I saw as virtues were for them probably only practical courses of action. In the end, I didn't know much about old women. Who does? They didn't know much about me either. That moral separation from others, which in me once had aroused mistrust and hardheartedness, afforded a new perspective on the dread of being swallowed up by love. What the *vecchia* taught me was to fear not vulnerability but the ice in my blood, the coldness toward others who are unlike me and toward the different boy within. Beneath the cover of otherness, old women, like young gay men disfigured by AIDS, were the semblance of the other in me.

These thoughts about old women come back to me as I recognize that my knowing Frank set new coordinates of love and death for me. Our partnership evolved from Frank's big-hearted response to Nellie and then Marie as indispensable to our spiritual seeking. Frank did not meet stricken Nellie for the first time as a boy of seven or eight observing his feeble grandmother. A boy's perspective is a glimpse from afar. Frank encountered Nellie's full-blown mental infirmity up close. A wounded healer himself, Frank watched and listened attentively so that he could feel what he could not hear in Nellie's silenced voice.

The holiday meal with Nellie, Marie, and Frank lifted my heart. Around the table breaking bread expressed a fellowship among one another and between us with the spirit of life. Unlike so many long, bleak winters, this season was a personal advent in Advent. A new arrival brought a futurity. In actual fact, a new family was beginning. Parts of my life that were incompatible were coming together for the first time. Better late than never.

In times of joy or distress, many people consult the Psalms for a wider perspective on experiencing delight or for guidance in handling anguish. My habit is to turn to *The Sayings of the Desert Fathers* and *The Forgotten Desert Mothers* for an understanding of life, especially the strength and responsibilities these solitaries found in aloneness. I feel strangely at home in their alien waste.

Reading about these Christian women and men of late antiquity was like peering through a looking glass; everything was new. Their lives were bold. They embraced aloneness as inescapable and sought release from enslavement to the world, even the religious world. They wanted the fullest possible freedom. Liberty for them meant a life oriented toward God as exemplified by Jesus in the gospel. To follow Jesus's perfect obedience to the commandment to love, the desert dwellers chose to live in solitude among the steppes and caves of Egypt, Syria, and Palestine, where they committed themselves to helping one another as essential to drawing closer to God. The great abbot Anthony summed up the life: "Our life and our death is with our neighbor." Gentle charity in the harshest imaginable conditions united them to all in spiritual seeking.

The elected aloneness of the desert dwellers addressed the seclusion I found imposed by illness or intolerance on people around me and on myself. The desert elders knew suffering. Abject physical hardship pervaded the third and fourth centuries. When famine and plague hit nearby towns, as regularly happened, the solitaries left their hermitage to care for the victims. They listened to the word; and more influentially, they did the word. In putting the word into action, the desert elders developed practices of caring that integrated prayer with deed into their daily life. Action became prayer.

I cannot do precisely what those women and men did. Their conditions in late-antique deserts are not mine in modern America. Christianity itself has changed, presenting new ways and afflictions to witness the gospel. For all my doubts and difficulties with the church, I saw hints, however partial and imperfect, of bringing the hermits' spare counsels to one another to practice in my efforts with Nellie's sickness. The solitaries' struggle for union with God articulated Nellie's deepest needs and my own effort to help the woman who had made me the object of her special care. My life and my death were with her.

Frank's joining us for the first time lent a soft grace to that Advent afternoon in Cedar Grove. The felt unity of love called to mind the blessing of caring for Nellie as constituent with being and of receiving a guest in ancient desert life. Hospitality was an important aspect of solitude. Seen by desert manners, the stranger was a reminder of humankind's status as traveler on earth, of our passing through a place—indeed, a world—that is not our own. The Christian solitaries, seeing the divine in the new arrival, received the guest in the name of God, which is to say in the name of love. Simple kindnesses, so crucial for survival in the ruthless desert, were sacred duties.

Nellie, who didn't respond to strangers, warmed to this new man who brought flowers to her desert world. It took time for her misaligned neurons to signal a response. Several months later, after Frank greeted Nellie with a kiss, the cone of silence under which she lived broke. Nellie lifted her head with a wide-eyed stare that poked through stillness to register something stronger than affection, and then piped, "Hello, Mister." Two words and a quick, slightly demented look sealed Frank's kinship. Her receptivity to kindness was another kind of youthfulness, of old age. While clogging arteries slowed the flow of blood to her brain, Frank's kindness opened a place in her heart for silent love. And with a collective knowing smile, we all came together in a Nellie moment. We savored plenitude in a flash.

Month after month, sickness and decrepitude cast Nellie into the barren places of life. There in secrecy, removed from the social world, she could still feel the power of the heart enlisted in the expanding service of grace. With Frank, we were now four who were alone together in an opaque world, and yet somehow more real. As one, we had Nellie's care in common. So much was new from so much that was lost in the daily tedious preparation for death. An Old World Italian American family, long without a father, who died in 1958, and buffeted by aging and illness, was on its way to becoming a modern family manqué held together by a gay partnership.

5

Entering My True Country

Give the body discipline and you will see that the body is for
the one who made it.

> —*The Forgotten Desert Mothers*

Sit in your cell, and your cell will teach you everything.

> —*The Sayings of the Desert Fathers*

To describe Frank only through his self-giving ways with Nellie and
Marie would offer too perfect a portrait of his character. Frank had
shadows. His struggles were fierce. From earliest childhood, he felt
ignored by his parents. The second of four children, he strained with
large and small gestures not to be overlooked. When he was three, and
his older brother, Lou, was to be the ring-bearer for his Uncle Angelo's
marriage to Enza, an Italian war-bride, Frank was desperate to be
dressed in a noticeable way comparable to his brother so as not to be
eclipsed. Not being seen meant lacking value.

Frank several times spoke of one episode. He was five. Uncle Carmine promised to take him to the beach on a summer day and never
showed up. The boy sat on the stoop waiting. Some children get over
the slight. Not Frank. The insult confirmed the inveterate fear of not
counting, of not being seen, of not being a member of the wedding.
Cruel disregard cast its long-lasting gloom. When he was eight, Frank
diligently stacked cans on shelves and cleaned the floor in his grandfather's grocery to gain affirmation. Appreciation came in the form
of more chores. Helpfulness didn't do the trick, any more than fine

clothes. Inside the adult Frank, that betrayed youngster still sits on the front steps of his house all dressed up and ready for the pleasure of the ocean, waiting for Uncle Carmine to think enough of his promise to pick him up. Young Frank learned early that things and people fail us. He was really waiting for God's attention by other names.

As visibility and recognition meant survival, being ignored triggered Frank's feeling of being cast off. Abandonment was his desert. Mirage followed mirage. Forever seeking to be seen, he missed seeing the strengths of modesty and gentleness that others admired in him. Never really finding in others the visibility that could come only from seeing himself, Frank felt erased. Nothing was ever given to him; he had to work for everything, especially love.

Resentment set in. I never forgot his recalling a crisis at thirteen. It was traumatic to hear. Anger nearly engulfed him in the telling. His mother was forty-two and pregnant with a child, her fourth, whom she could not handle and did not want. Her spurning life at its source in her womb sharpened Frank's sensitivity to rejection, both of him and others. He begged his mother to deliver and keep her child. Never mothered, the teenage Frank became mother to his mother. He cooked, cleaned, consoled, and cajoled. Then he became mother again. The baby brother, who was born, was emotionally Frank's child. They remain close.

By instinct, Frank knew the ropes of mothering. He got caught in their trap. The snare set by this hurried responsibility sapped the time and energy that should have gone to growing up and schoolwork. The result was a mediocre performance in high school that further dimmed his self-image. Yet through mothering he has retained his natural playfulness. Frank should have been a daddy.

From those early years looking, Frank turned to the church for confirmation. Where he sought goodness, he found aggressive duplicity and dogma used as agencies for oppression. Where he sought community, he found heightened loneliness. Ordination made him less a servant of the Lord than a cog in a clerical bureaucracy. When he suffered the humiliation of seeking dignity in an impersonal power system, Frank was left alone with his confused emotions.

Of all the pain that the church inflicted on Frank, the most sustained was the repudiation of his true identity. Religion can do that. His pastoral virtues were inseparable from his sexuality, which he had to disguise into a fake self which impersonated the judgmental authority that disowned him. Even sexually inactive, as he was, he was deemed harboring "an intrinsic disorder." Deeply harmful to all gay men and lesbians, Catholic Christianity's view of homosexuality weighed down those already trying to live by their ordination vows. They were on the run from shame and living a lie. Frank concealed his true self. In Frank, battling the disgrace of being gay stripped away whatever confidence he had as a minister. His clerical superiors had no idea that he was gay. Parishioners who esteemed him for his warmth also never knew him as gay. Had they done so, they would have learned about God's unpredictably rich creativeness.

Frank's search for the true ground of his identity mirrored my confusion. I too was looking in the wrong places for confirmation. I could not help but seek the world's recognition. The lures were neat and clear. Research, publication, promotion, status, and salary made me feel worthy and gave me permission to be gay and openly gay with colleagues, but something was always missing. My sense was that I would not need the fleeting approval of the world if I had attention from a life beyond myself. That essential reliance on something ultimate, I believe, explains the appeal that elderly women in my family held. Being sustained by the very font of life, by God alone, was what I saw in dying old women.

Frank and I had to grow, bit by bit and reluctantly, into knowledge of ourselves that was always changing and destabilizing us. It was amazing how little, despite all the rapport of passion and commitment, how little Frank and I understood each other at first and how much the unfinished work of love would involve my capacitated mother, and eventually my willful sister and Frank's irascible mother.

Dealing with inner deprivation was a career in itself for Frank. Feelings of never being intellectually or morally good enough nagged him. The constant beneath the self-doubts in Frank's life was his talent to be a man for others, his good and true vocation. He was Johnny-on-the-spot when someone needed a ride to the doctor, a trip to the supermarket, or a visit. Never was there an ulterior motive, unless satisfaction in leaving a situation better than one found it can be called selfish.

Beneath his cheerful round of doing for others, a heartrending drama of inner turmoil played out. Frank had a tentative and susceptible sense of himself. He wanted to count before people and God. I speak for him now in words close to his own—and not far off from my yearning. If no one else loved him, God at least would. Then he could accept himself.

Frank's ingenuously stated yearning brought out my ambivalence about God and divine favor. God's reward sometimes did not seem like reward at all. His gift seemed more a demand for sacrifice and deeper duties of service. As Frank knew better than most, God's presence can be bitter. It can stop the heart, can turn events on a dime. What, then, do we mean by love of God? What does such affection, if it is affection, feel like when one is being nailed to a crossbeam or inhaling gas in Auschwitz shower rooms? Being gay hardly felt like a blessing or grace gift. Why must gay persons hide their sexuality? In daily living the price of love was life itself. Whatever the cost, however God's love would come, Frank awaited it. Such incessant waiting had to be endlessly painful.

Frank's pain came through early in our relationship. About two months after we met, Frank was still working for the chaplaincy council in New Jersey and couldn't wait to jump-start a different career. Work anchored his self-esteem. Prospects were few. Studying for the priesthood had not prepared Frank to hunt for a job in business. Without a future, he felt that he lacked a stable identity. We had spent this particular Saturday afternoon at the Union Square market looking for crisp Double Jonathan apples with a pineapple-like center that were grown by an upstate orchard. The small pleasures of the market's aromatic fresh bread and multicolored chrysanthemums eluded him that day. He talked about being between worlds. Families, couples, and single persons going from stand to stand buying fruit and vegetables reminded him that he was not part of the domestic life for which the crowd was shopping. In fact, he felt that he didn't have any life at all.

When we returned to the apartment, where Frank was free to open up, his suppressed emotions erupted with urgency over his inability to fit in with society or the church. His sense of being apart made him despondent. Frank did not hold back expressing what he was looking for. "I want a new life," he said, "even if that means driving a truck." When written down, his words really should be interspersed with downward-moving spaces to catch the reflective pauses in his voice. I don't know how to record the sinking force in his voice.

Frank's soft-spoken appeal blindsided me. I was like a deer caught full in the eyes by headlights. Feelings of alienation, to be sure, had previously come up in many forms between us. How could they not? We understood from the beginning that our work of love as gay men was to make for each other a place that society did not provide. But Frank was seeking a far greater security on a deeper ground than any human bond could forge. God had to be the basis for his individual and partnered identity. However he lived, he wanted it to be by the will of God. That command, he felt certain, was to be found amid the confusion and repudiation around us. Though I knew Frank was right, I resisted his clarity because such a measure of human worth guaranteed that I would fail.

Frank was open about his very being. His exposure revealed not a new area of knowledge about life but unacknowledged disturbances in me. I was unable to express sympathy easily. To avoid deeper zones of contact, I fled from life to books, from passion to abstraction. My mind tried to handle what my heart could not. Did Frank have St. Paul's "new man" or Kierkegaard's idea of the dialectical self in mind? Why would anyone want to be other than who she or he is? Could one become another self? To my mind, Frank's not being a part of social and religious institutions was a sign of integrity, not a condition to be overcome.

Frank put into words what I felt but could not. In retrospect, I sensed then a link between my being with Frank and going across the river to Nellie. It took strength to care for a dying mother in the same way that it took strength to stand by a searching lover without façades. Both mother and lover presented a vulnerability that threatened to tear away defenses that I was shoring up. In my carefully constructed buffered state, I was too weak to be loved.

Frank knew that he was lost; he was dissatisfied with what he had; he complained; he was angry; he was bereft; and he sought a new direction. These were goads honestly to find a way out of his aloneness. Deliverance from his broken self may never come, but his tortuous passage was humanizing. The dreadful place in which he was stranded revealed the heart of a man able to withstand the trials to which he was subjected. Through knowledge of his deficiencies, Frank drew decency from a hostile context, gentleness from abandonment. He who was never at home in the social or ecclesiastical world received the exile's gift of courage to endure the wilderness of God. He was wistful for faith but not secure in it. Even as believer, Frank knew he couldn't belong to the church. Long before the federal government sought a degree of intolerance with the "don't ask, don't tell" guideline for members of the armed services, the church had the ironclad rule "come out, go out" for its clergy. The universal church secured its borders with armed guards around the contested territory of homosexuality.

Frank did fit in my family by making Nellie and Marie his own without fuss. His passion for work found endless opportunities to leave things better than he found them. He helped put a new roof on their house, planted tulips along the driveway, and fixed the kitchen cabinets. He was the soul of kindness with Nellie. It made him feel good to know that he could keep her as comfortable as possible. Amiable and prone to playfulness, he also brought lightheartedness into a weary house of sickness. For a family whose humor would a fit in matchbox that was already full, his making fun of things redressed our undue solemnity.

He knew when and how to curb my edgy impatience with my mother and sister. A cautionary glance from Frank that asked, "Are you helping matters?" or "Is this necessary?" checked the irritation he saw rising in me toward my sister, whose small requests for help sometimes struck me as inordinate demands on my time. He showed me that his teasing, which I found hostile, was a way of including as well excluding. His skill of doing matched his way of observing and listening. Others around him felt that they were heard and understood, even if they weren't.

There was no end to Frank's material and emotional renewals in the lives around him because there was no end to his need for making himself new. He persevered. If his repairs around the Giannone house in Cedar Grove did not get him the new self he sought, Nellie and Marie nevertheless benefited from Frank's improvements and personal attention. Frank never talked about what he did. I doubt that he even thought about his helping efforts.

At the heart of Frank's struggle was an inborn sense of love that differed radically from what modern culture promoted as love. Not only popular magazines and television commercials but also religion represented love as protective, making us feel good as well as worthy to be loved in return.

For Frank, love was a matter of the will. Emotion inevitably entered into this love but was less important than the duty he felt to love. This sense of being obliged to love was an emanation of his character. His gentle disposition made him more exposed than comfortable with others because his quiet strength could, in our aggressive world, come off as weakness. In fact, people presumed on his trust and willingness to help. He felt the slights. And he remained loyal.

While Frank struggled inwardly, I drifted along driven by academic satisfactions. Though he was supportive of my work, Frank's example showed me that professional rewards of publication and promotion, useful in themselves, were ornaments of a constructed self. My life was forged in the dread of the responsibilities of being gay and in the refusal directly to grapple with the inner person I was meant to be. Rhetorically smooth manuscripts masked the jagged life formed by razor-sharp thorns during decisive years.

As a gay boy growing up in New Jersey during and after World War II, I learned that homosexuality was not simply a matter of emotional perversion; it carried the stigma of moral degeneracy. It contaminated the community and undermined the family. The only known remedy was to root out the pestiferous toxin so that it does not spread. One point on which society and church were in full agreement was that a homosexual could not be tolerated. Being gay felt like a capital offense.

During World War II, the federal government classified and discriminated against American women and men on the basis of their homosexuality, excluding them from military service. If discovered as gay serving in the ranks, they were discharged without honor and consequently denied the generous benefits of the G.I. Bill. Getting a job with a dishonorable discharge was tough. Discrimination went deep. President Dwight D. Eisenhower's 1953 executive order excluded homosexuals from working in civilian agencies too. The order required private companies with government contracts to search out and fire homosexual employees. Joseph McCarthy reigned. Professed Catholic and self-styled patriot, the senator embodied in the extreme the damages of institutionalized homophobia. Fanaticism ratified and extended his self-hatred.

Until I came to New York at the age of thirty-two, in August 1967, I shared my gay identity with only a few close friends. That's the way it was then, before Stonewall: Get a job, keep it, survive the dangers of gay life—blackmail, loss of job, street beatings, religious censure, arrest, countless forms of legal harassment, and murder. Safety trumped freedom. I lived, worked, and prayed in fear. I certainly could neither respect nor trust authorities.

With HIV on the rise in the late 1970s, gay loathers from pulpit and television screen typecast gay men as cartoonish disease carriers and agents of social breakdown. Homosexuality held terror. Pitchforks were sharpened. To defend itself against the imagined satans, an un-Christian Catholicism competed with an un-Christian fundamentalist Christianity in America for the medal of intolerance. Of all the banes assailing faith, homosexuality was the most heinous. Clerical magistrates of the old-time American religion of vengeance, good servants of God, knew that the remedy was extirpation.

In some quarters Christianity was ready with bland declarations about injustice, usually after the people prodded and embarrassed leaders and bishops about inequality; but Christianity, tragically, was never a creative force in social action to support the civil rights of homosexuals. Instead their homophobic scorn projected into the larger culture.

An immigrant Catholic church, to cite one source of derision, was joined at the hip with conservative American thought, which Catholicism yearned to be a part of. In 1997 when society was becoming more open, the American bishops recognized gays as "always our children"; but never, even as the country was becoming more tolerant, did they weigh in on the debate to protect their children by repealing the "don't ask, don't tell" policy. The bishops didn't care. Lifting high the cross rivaled flag-waving. By keeping company with homophobia, holy callousness and political bigotry wiped blood on each other's hands.

Though my allegiance was with the activists who challenged the religious right and demanded recognition and medical interventions, breaking away from my shell was not political. I joined a small prayer group at St. Joseph's Church on Sixth Avenue. Also, I was more attentive to helping Marie care for Nellie as a way of keeping me busy and away from the dangers of gay life. I sought an emotional sanctuary. I was useful, somewhere.

Over time, looking after a feeble mother in her late seventies and eighties took my measure. Some lessons were amusingly basic, as when dressing Nellie I learned that women buttoned blouses right-to-left, unlike men who fastened shirts in reverse. Tougher truths were inescapable. Try as I did, I couldn't change Nellie's soiled clothes and bed sheets with only good intentions. Physical care was messy, its rewards elusive. If I looked for thanks, all I found was another set of soiled pajamas to launder. Being with Nellie required virtues that opposed egotism, timetable, and regulation. I had a schedule of buses and classes; Nellie had a leaky bladder. My plans and self-concern were always warring in me against the self-forgetting needed to manage the smells and flimsiness of her body.

Very much Nellie's child, I was afraid of getting close to people, especially to her dying. Loving thy neighbors in the family meant leaving them alone. The thoughts of the heart were too dangerous to express candidly. All my life, distance allowed me to manage fear, pain, sin, and struggles with familial expectations. I tried to avoid disappointment by expecting little from them. Without knowing it, I was running the risk of developing a tightly involuted self-concern. My tendency to keep a distance certainly wounded Frank, whose love was forcing me to feel in exposed ways.

Pressure on me to change came from another direction. During Nellie's last four or five years, the range of her movement and emotions narrowed. Gradually the hushed space she occupied admitted only soft responses from me. Her repose filtered out my impatience. One morning as I helped her from bed to the bathroom, her baby steps seemed more tentative and wobbly than usual. Then while Nellie was standing naked and holding on to the towel rack after a bowel movement, her spindly legs were caving in as I sponged her buttocks. With one arm catching her, all I did was drench the floor with soapy water. Frustrated, I said to Nellie, "Hold tight. You're making it hard for me." My scolding immediately echoed in my heart. Each syllable struck like a dull blow against my foolishness. *Hard for me?* I was too mortified to say, "Forgive me." Dementia made Nellie anger-proof, protected her beyond my words. I had to rely on a shared physical and visual language that we built together in her solitude.

One would have thought that caring for a stricken mother left no room for pride, but that was not the case. Pride in me ranged from believing that I could manage Nellie best on my own to feeling anger that others in the family didn't pitch in. The focus on myself had a power to cast unselfish acts into the shade and deprive them of love.

Haphazard duties bound Nellie and me. Little tasks held a force that was altering my life. Like Frank, I was groping toward a new life, but without his conscious expression of needing one. If as the gospel promises, we could encounter the divine in daily lives, then the closest I had come to that possibility over fifty decades was with Nellie in her illness. If I was bumping into God, the jolt came through Nellie's repeated pulling me away from myself and into her irregular bodily needs.

If God was actively present, God for me was an event. Not an incident with clear disclosure. *Event* may be too strong a word. It was an occasion with uncertain hint. Belief, to the degree that I dare use the word, was an intuition that contact with Nellie sparked—and quickly receded, that and nothing more. The experience was an inexplicable presentiment that useful service made me part of a whole. If the church did not lead me to the feet of God, washing Nellie's hammer-toes guided me to the need of another person. For that moment, I was no longer myself. I was not the visiting son or surrogate sister or mother. I was the stricken old woman, her weariness of spirit. The Nellie instant was fleeting and lonely. The experience of freedom I called God. I found myself moving out of the safe and familiar and into—well, somewhere else.

The feeling of freedom invariably gave way to a mood of restriction. There was the challenge just to return physically each week, often two or three times a week, to Cedar Grove and Nellie's increasing frailty. I dragged my feet. I didn't want to be coffined in the house of guilt and sorrow. My familiar foreign home got smaller and tighter and airless. The expectation of Nellie's death closed in on me. The fact of her death brought a sense of futility. I found helplessness a traumatic emotion to manage. It was like feeding the winds. Feeling useless was a temptation to throw up my hands before great odds. I began grinding my teeth. Futility was another evil to be fought with my meager ordnance of wanting to see Nellie to the grave.

Self-respect sometimes conquered selfishness. Neglecting Nellie was beneath me. Nellie was my own. Caring for one's own was taking care of oneself. After all these women did for me, duty and loyalty were sacred. Where humility failed, pride succeeded in lending a helping hand.

I wish that I could have tended Nellie with the deep humility that avails one to God's aid. Then I could have abided in him who said, "Fear not, I am with you." I had no idea what the experience of divine support was or that I would know it when it happened. Still and all, I wanted the divine hand to be as touchable as Nellie's bony, twisted fingers.

My part-time mothering life sharpened my sense of floundering in radical inadequacy. I consistently felt without resource, on my own, before the mortal enemy. Foolishly, instead of acknowledging my weakness, I sought to control the ravages of Nellie's illness and allay her unseen discomfort. My efforts ran up against the fact that Nellie was always there, constantly changing, at all times deteriorating. I kept on kicking boulders. I tried to deal with the messiness of sickness through small precisions, wiping her runny eyes and dribbling mouth. In the end, illness has it own objective, and it is continually wielding its advantage of being unknowable.

Fear drew me into denying that Nellie would die on my watch. Though her death would free me from the burden of traveling from Manhattan to New Jersey and the frustrating job of nursing, I welcomed the sight of Nellie's breathing, stick-thin body. I was afraid that losing her would freshen the ordeal of mourning, already opened by the great trial of AIDS. It was easier to deal with her debility than with her death. The routine of being with her served as a defense against the invading truth of my own dying.

Most of the time, mothering meant watching. Vigilance afforded a vantage to see a new basis of comfort. The frailty of Nellie's body that alarmed onlookers appeared to have the opposite effect on her. Slow physical loss put Nellie at her ease. Her diminishing body trained her spirit to surrender. She appeared to take in the losses and suffering of her condition with a quiet capacity to release them in the form of a still presence. Observing her, I was finding out the great worth of the useless. Nellie just rested. She breathed in vulnerability and breathed out tenderness. I, by contrast, gasped for air. Because my spirit was too frail to do the work of grief, I frequently exhaled annoyance and fatigue. Still, the old woman's body remained before me as a source of wisdom whenever my heart was open enough to take its revelations. Nellie's dying offered a standpoint from which to observe the reeling confusion of living, of living as a gay man during the HIV crisis.

Was there a place that transformed dying and caring for the dying into fruitfulness? The ancient desert mothers and fathers of Egypt and Palestine believed there was. They held out the hope of finding such an atmosphere of spiritual liberty in the very meekness enforced by the unremitting diminution of dying. They spoke of humility as a place of living and learning: "Humility is the land where God wants us to go and offer sacrifice." The land to which they were summoned is the desert.

There was no doubt that I had to learn the lessons taught in the desert. The desert is more than an arid, poor place. The desert is what the desert feels like. The directive to the dry land issued from Nellie's withering body. A senile mother was teaching her bookish son about yielding to love by accepting bodily affliction. On the mornings when I sat with her in the bathroom waiting to bathe her, I was with a poor, banished child of Eve. Before me were her sunken eyes and pencil-thin ankles. She was the meek. She was the poor. Though she did not cry out, she was the way.

My reading and writing about Flannery O'Connor helped illume the way that Nellie's deteriorating body set out before me. O'Connor lived with the systemic ravages of lupus and its haywire hormonal treatments from twenty-six until she died at thirty-nine. Disease forced her to go back home to rural Georgia, from which she'd fled. With typical self-humor, she called herself "a hermit novelist." Compulsory physical retirement, strangely enough, was the condition in which her artistic greatness and wisdom flourished.

O'Connor understood illness as both a bodily condition and a spiritual site, each with a mysterious journey. She described the complex topography of illness with stark accuracy. "I have never been anywhere but sick," O'Connor wrote in 1956, eight years before her death in August 1964. "In a sense sickness is a place, more instructive than a long trip to Europe, and it's always a place where there's no company, where nobody can follow." The isolation imposed by illness was for O'Connor a school for life, death, and her art—an art that burns with searing truths about the aching body inducing spiritual yearnings for God. Writing from inside the experience of protracted sickness, O'Connor, a modern desert mother, revealed a humility that accepted terminal illness as grace sent from God. "Sickness before death is a very appropriate thing and I think those that don't have it miss one of God's mercies."

I for one was and remain happy to pass up such hard terms of clemency, but in that place where I would not be lied to I knew that sickness would meet me some day. Then, like Nellie in her years of sickness, I will meet and need the divine. In the meantime, I was going where Nellie was taking me.

Nellie the émigré child in displaced old age was experiencing an inner migration toward life, the source of life.

No one would be more surprised than Nellie to find herself running into God, much less receiving his help. In fact my mother had turned her back squarely on him more than fifty years before, when her eldest of four children, Florence, died at sixteen in 1937 after an elective appendectomy. Nellie gave birth to Florence when she was twenty. After difficult formative years, fragmented and full of toil that led to her dropping out of high school, Nellie had a new beginning as young mother. Florence was the child of Nellie's youth, child of her hope and years to come, and most fortunately female. Nellie, the immigrant girl, laid her own unlived youth on Florence. Mother and daughter grew up together.

The summer of 1937 shattered that bond. Very early on the morning of July 30, 1937, a hospital nurse called Nellie and my father, Salvatore, and told them to come immediately to Presbyterian Hospital in Newark. They took the new cotton dress with puffy sleeves that Nellie made to celebrate their daughter Florence's return home and found her dead. The dead child left loneliness in the family. It was an empty house, an empty womb, and empty world. Florence's death was slaying my mother's heart. She chose a burial site next to the outer fence at a nearby cemetery so that she could visit the grave whenever she wanted. For several years after Florence's death, my mother without saying a word walked from our house to the cemetery fence. She took me along by the hand, maybe to steady her or just to have someone to cling to. I was five and six then. At my father's order, my sister Marie followed us.

Bereft of her mothering daughter, Nellie at thirty-seven felt orphaned. Like Grandma, Nellie lost her mother, her mothering daughter. The violation of her love made Nellie's blood run cold. Her healthy child's sudden death at sixteen was a body blow to whatever faith Nellie had. She knew who hit her and responded in kind. Never again would Nellie have anything to do with him. God was disappointment. He was a cold negation of her hopes. He was not welcome in her home.

But he kept Nellie in mind. I couldn't help but consider that Nellie, who snubbed God, was undergoing the mercy of divine mothering. If God was pressing Nellie in his arms, divine grace acted in her body as her arteries systematically closed the flow of blood to her vital organs. She hardly uttered sounds, took fewer steps. Only vague outlines of people and objects registered on her optic nerves. Her appetite waned. Each physical loss bent the fierce will by which she lived for decades into a new obedience to the dependency in which she finally lived.

There were indications of Nellie's inner change. She neither resisted nor complained. For her daily need to be cleaned, clothed, and fed, she relied on Marie, Frank's Friday and Saturday visits, and my regular assistance. Gradually, a calm settled on Nellie that suggested an interior support at the root of her being that was greater than that provided by her children's helping hands.

There were probably neurological explanations for a certain euphoria's setting in when parts of the brain stop functioning. All of that may have been true but was not the deeper truth. The late-antique hermits offered another way to see Nellie. The desert mothers and fathers spoke of feeling free from care when in their solitude they came to depend entirely on God, the one power that did not fail them, the one in whom they hoped and placed their trust. I wondered if the long stretches of Nellie's peacefulness shared in that freedom. To be sure, Nellie had moved beyond fear. She was free simply to be. Thanks to past thriftiness aided by Marie's management and her teaching career, neither lacked financial means; but Nellie bore a poverty of space, of mobility, of community, of health. Certainly, Nellie's poverty recommended her to the protector of the lonely and obscured poor.

Poverty was very much in the air one breathed around Nellie. I belonged to her poverty. Her neediness revealed my poverty of patience and service. Whatever I did seemed insufficient. Caring required more attention and emotional staying power than I imagined or had. The dearth of my efforts not only spoke for what Nellie could not verbalize about her experience; it helped to explain what Nellie was doing for me. She showed that one could live fully on the bare minimum if one had divine support. She taught me about abandonment. She pointed me to the place where there's no company, where no one could follow. Nellie was the first of several burdens that became my need.

To be with Nellie presented the choice either of being clinically detached from her relentless losses or of submitting myself to her impoverishment. Although I feared losing myself in her estrangement, I was nudged toward a renunciation of wanting to have my own way. Nellie and I both underwent a forced dispossession of our private will, she through her body and me through a power I couldn't identify. I thought of free choice as a single force, but it is a convergence of many and conflicting wishes. Somewhere buried beneath my self-will I was receptive to learning from her dependency the rudiments of compassion. I couldn't take away her suffering.

I have had always to struggle against myself. In 1985 when Nellie's decline took a steep turn, I was fifty-one years old. Time was short for me too, and my sense of inadequacy was long. I was aware of having done little to serve others, including Frank, who, four years into our relationship, had freely given himself to Nellie simply by doing what had to be done without thinking about results.

I wanted results. That was another trap. Being with chronically ill Nellie infected me with the disease of futility. Nothing was ever finished. It was one thing to feel that what I did was not quite done and yet another to feel that those imperfect efforts had no value. The sense of uselessness was debilitating. The antidote was satisfaction in the smallest tasks, such as changing her nightclothes, giving prescribed medication that probably did nothing for her, and wiping the saliva flow from her mouth so she would eat the slice of Kraft yellow cheese I unwrapped for her lunch. Contentment was brief. I had to understand that the distance between what I wanted and what I got done with Nellie was not a defeat of service or trust. It gauged the boundaries of our being. At this remove, failures, the daily bread of caregiving, were occasions to reflect on losses and to get ready for them.

During the week, I took public transportation. On weekends, when Frank didn't have to drive to work, we took his car to New Jersey. One late Sunday, when Frank and I drove from Cedar Grove back home to the West Village, he typically offered cautions about my impatience.

Occasionally appealing to my limited sense of humor, he suggested that I let go the anxiety of the moment and move on to the next worry. Invariably, Frank was blunt. With stern sympathy, he encouraged me see that part of caring for Nellie was to persevere in a sense of failure. He reminded me also that I could leave the house of sickness, whereas Marie could not take a bus or hop into a car with a partner who would hear her out on the way home. Frank reminded me to think of Marie's predicament. Marie had to stay behind. Day in and day out, Marie found as best she could a way to live in a place that had no reference point other than senescence. Sunday evening after Sunday evening driving back to our home was a time to take stock of those defeats. There we were, Jersey boys, born in Newark and Belleville, made in Greenwich Village, being remade in Jersey. Marie remained in Jersey. For all our wanderings, we were never far from New Jersey.

My Sunday brooding calls to mind the poet Wallace Stevens's thought on the Lord's Day. On Sunday, while people of traditional faith attend their various churches, Stevens recounts his "Sunday Morning" in a private ceremony. He portrays his soul's reflections through a woman in her prime. She is relaxed at home in her dressing gown having late-morning coffee when death intrudes on her repose. Mature, she accepts the "sure obliteration" of her life. At the same time, she honors her "need for some imperishable bliss." Theological abstraction doesn't answer her yearning. "Divinity must live within herself." Her mind turns to the outdoors. Changing weather, shifting colors, and animated creatures hearten the woman. At evening her meditation ends as she watches flocks of pigeons in the sky. They are casually rippling downward to darkness, gliding smoothly to death and the boundless source of life's infinitude of possibilities.

Many Sunday evenings I hitched a ride on the "extended wings" of these common birds. On their wind, I set off eastward to the Palestine of heart from which Stevens's poem issues and to which the woman's meditation returns. Before going to bed, I turned from the sayings of the desert teachers to the recollections for Sunday evening in *The Prayer of the Church* for help through the night and ensuing days with

dying Nellie. After scriptural readings, the concluding prayer was forever the same. *May the Lord Bless us, may he keep us from all evil
and lead us to life everlasting.* The onerous and trivial duties of caring
wouldn't change. It was a matter of doing my part and leaving the rest
to life and the Lord.

Richard and Nellie, Newark, N.J., 1940

Richard and his parents, First Holy Communion, 1941

Marie, high school graduation, 1942

Aunt Emma and Richard, Confirmation, 1947

Marie in Stratford, Conn., 1956

Richard and Nellie,
Providence, R.I., 1958

Richard in Trieste,
Italy, as a Fulbright
Fellow, 1961

Richard and Nellie, South Bend, Ind., 1962

Richard on East 19th Street, New York, 1967, just after moving to the city

Richard with
Nellie on her
seventy-fifth
birthday,
1975

Nellie in Cedar
Grove, N.J., 1978

Nellie in the driveway of her and Marie's home on Harper Terrace, Cedar Grove, N.J., 1970s

Richard in Charlemont, Mass., 1977

Richard at Sage Chapel, Cornell University, 1983

Jane Street

Marie, 1978

Above: Marie and Nellie in Cedar Grove, N.J., 1985

Below: St. Joseph's Church on Sixth Avenue

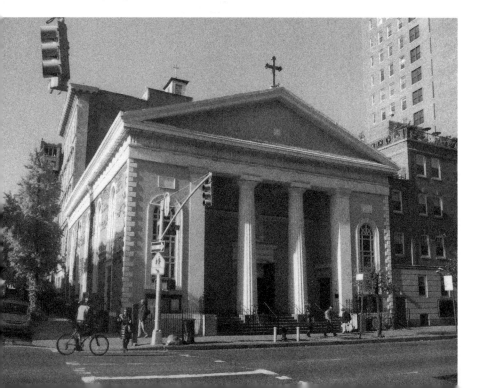

Frank and Richard, Jerusalem, R.I., 1992

Richard teaching at
Fordham, 2007 (Photo
by Bruce Gilbert/
Fordham University)

Richard and Frank, Jerusalem, R.I., 2009

6

Love's Hiding Places

The darker the mystery, the more we are illumined by it. So a simple soul finds God where he seems not to appear.

—Jean-Pierre de Caussade, *Abandonment to Divine Providence*

Frank and I lived in the West Village without leading the recognizable Greenwich Village life set by classless bohemians or pop-hip gay men representing the newest iterations of cool and who, let's face it, would find us boring. We had little to do with aging Village lefties who clung to their landmark causes and rent-controlled apartments. We had even less in common with *arriviste* bond traders, trust-fund kids, and the predecessors of "Sex and the City" wannabes who were colonizing the neighborhood.

Inconspicuous, graying middle-aged gay men, Frank and I shared more with the concerns of unassuming women caregivers in suburban New Jersey. Accustomed to being apart, we found on Jane Street, all the same, a relaxed niche among the ascending social and political energies, all of which left lots of room for the two of us to go our own way and concentrate on personal tasks. That we did.

Our trans-Hudson trek by bus and car discreetly moved through the gentrifying hum and buzz encircling us. When the city's fondness for redeveloping the seedy into dilapidated panache moved from SoHo and Tribeca to the meatpacking district, fashion continually redefined our unexceptional 750 square feet on the corner of Hudson and Jane streets. The bustle actually nourished the routines of our life. On days off from classes during the week, I continued to walk thirty blocks up clanging Eighth Avenue to Gate 405 at the unruly Port Authority Terminal at 40th Street for a morning bus to Cedar Grove. Somnambulant suits with briefcases got off in New York to make room for Hispanic day laborers and black domestic workers with heavy eyes and me to board for New Jersey suburbs. All were too tired to break the early slump with talk or even visual contact. On weekends Frank and I drove out to see his parents in Belleville and then to my mother and sister. When we returned to Jane Street, finding a parking space in the area got harder because of the crowds coming to the fashion-forward hangouts and geek-chic clubs, but its renewing vitality welcomed us home and freed us to become who we essentially were. We were mothering sons. By the rule of Village insouciance, that was just another unremarkable way of being in the mix. To feel the ordinariness of marginality is to stake a small claim to fitting in.

I channeled subcultures, from the Village to western Essex Country, from hip milieu to straight context, from the Bronx to teach and then to the city for a partnered gay life. Meaning came from what I was doing and where I was doing it at the time. This fluid identity served me well. I was spared being defined by surroundings. As a gay man with a partner and a duty to a dying mother, I felt released from the coercive models oppressing the gay as well as the straight world. With Frank, I didn't have to be Tweedledum to Tweedledee following the regimented Village trail. Social markers didn't gauge the progress or failure of our partnership.

Although I believed firmly that the same human love had the same human rights, I had reservations about the social institution of marriage with its emotional and legal proscriptions as setting partners up for failure. The arguments for same-sex marriage are compelling. Health insurance, taxes, basic justice, and the psychological component of belonging are reasons enough to mobilize for a fair shake under the law. Marriage is fine for those who believe it will do them practical good. Loyalty for me, however, is not tied to cultural sanction. An anarchist prompting in me, which allows people to be different, distrusts institutions and governments. Actually, the contemporary push for marriage equality could shift the work of love from how loyalty feels and works to how the partnership appears and satisfies the marketable norm. Marriage could then boomerang if gay partners emulate patterns and expectations that oppress heterosexual spouses. Assigned roles for Frank and me had long since lost their usefulness. We passed or failed muster as our love deepened or fell short. Success was felt in bending our personal will to the need of the other and God. In the Catholic ceremony the two partners married each other, and that we did. The minister merely witnesses.

Frank and I did register as domestic partners in New York City for any protection that the document gave us. My main concerns were hospital visitation rights and medical decisions. Officially partnered, we still had very limited standing under the law and no place whatever in the Catholic church into which we had both been baptized and yet did not share in the dignity of the baptized. While I write these words, I don't feel anger. Weary exhaustion accepts institutional rebuff as one of Christianity's numerous contradictions of its vaunted religious principles.

And I must say, too, that being cut off from the church had its own compensation. Frank and I did not confuse prescribed pieties with the approval our true nature needed. Faith, to be authentic for me, had to escape all religious descriptions. The way of one, or two, to draw close to God, is not the way for all. The actual work before us with Nellie and our personal struggle offered us more than did the church; it held the imprimatur of love. I'm not sure that I loved God, but I was willing to live by my duties to Nellie, Marie, and Frank.

Above and beyond helping Nellie in dementia's shadows, I lived in the full political light of day where I was also tried by the heart—not as a mothering son but as nursing brother to men with HIV. The last four years of Nellie's life, 1982 through 1986, witnessed the crumbling of the sexual freedoms gained in the '60s and '70s by the gay liberation movement. HIV/AIDS was the latest installment in the human story of banishment and captivity. The retrovirus pillaged the gardens of earthly delights into grounds of anguish. Back rooms of gay bars, bathhouses, truck depots on Washington Street, and the empty piers that were docking places for orgies along the Hudson River lay in ruins. We all lived in the place described by the Israelites as swarming with locusts and portrayed by Christian desert-dwellers as lurking with unseen predators. The ancient killers morphed into skin-crawling microbes roving as the gay plague, unseen, like the teeming desert demons. The locusts swarming the biblical desert finally vanished when the godsend of climate and temperature restrained the migrating insects. The primitive hermits subdued their demons with prayer.

But nothing stopped the random progression of HIV devouring its prey. The expanding HIV wasteland was a chastening reminder of the reality of danger, hardship, and death that was forgotten in the sexual spree. The insidious pestilence called for direct action. By the late 1980s, the time arrived to ACT UP. Playwright-provocateur Larry Kramer, with a gay machismo all his own, did just that with a call to arms in March 1987 at the Lesbian and Gay Community Service Center on 13th Street. If President Reagan thought people were getting severe colds that would go away as they came, residents of Greenwich Village could tell by Mother Teresa's sending Third World Missionaries of Love from Calcutta to open a shelter off swinging Christopher Street on Greenwich Street that desolation was at hand and here to stay. It went without saying that medical facts, research, drugs, and education were crucial to treat and prevent the disease. Gay men rallied with impressive speed and political effectiveness. The AIDS Coalition to Unleash Power took on Big Pharma's greedy control through patent protections of HIV medications to demand lower prices and equitable distribution and to gain access to experimental therapies. Combative members of the movement broke into the New York Stock Exchange to protest the exorbitant price of the one approved AIDS drug.

Like the Freedom Riders of the early 1960s who challenged racism in the Deep South, ACT UP with the weapons of civil disobedience fought the entrenched sexism in religious institutions. I did not join the Act Uppers in the line of fire. As they demonstrated on the steps and inside of St. Patrick's Cathedral and then were dragged off en masse into waiting police vans, I watched them on the evening news. Detachment from political activism grew out of the self-censoring I adopted in early years to make peace with homosexuality. But I never made peace with being a guilty bystander. Caution came at a price. My judgments about politics and literature were not entirely my own. HIV, however, was loosening the chains of orthodoxy in the way I lived and taught.

During the epidemic, I was comfortable being openly gay in the English Department at Fordham. Colleagues were free of homophobia and outspoken about encouraging the new approaches of gay studies and queer theory. I also began to feel more relaxed in conferences with students. On one occasion, a graduate student came to my office for an extension of the deadline for his final research paper, but he was clearly asking for something more. He looked me straight in the eye and said he'd just learned that he was HIV-positive and couldn't concentrate on anything else.

Professors make a point of being intellectual, never psychological, advisors. The student's candor honored me. I crossed the line and stayed on the other side of the professional divide. I closed the office door, took him in my arms, and gave him the phone number of a physician who had an extensive gay practice. I listened to the young man in that particular way one shares in an unburdening. I was feeling the feeling to which I reacted. For neither the first nor the last time, devastating news shook me to the foundation of the deepest hope in which my soul dwells. When I respond from that inner place, as I did with the student, my voice feels authentic and free of the self-censoring that goes with being a gay instructor. For the record, I want to add that the young man finished his doctorate, got a job, and found his partner. The last I heard, they planned on having a child with a surrogate mother.

Students helped me to be more myself in the classroom as well. A discussion of James Baldwin's *Giovanni's Room* exemplified a breaking-through. Baldwin's 1956 novel dramatizes the sexual paranoia of a handsome American drifter in Europe. In Paris he falls in love with another foreigner, an Italian barman and also bisexual but comfortable in his newfound love. Being gay, however, brings the young American down. By the late 1980s, thanks to feminism and cultural studies, every topic was open for discussion in class. Speaking from a post-Stonewall sensibility, the students responded with impressive acuity. They took physical attraction between men as true and rightful, and they understood how love could reconcile Baldwin's lovers from the feeling of being strangers in a strange land.

The estrangement of the foreign lovers spoke to young people. They brought an intensely focused, highly charged response to *Giovanni's Room*. For them the importance of the American's torment arose less from sexual desire than from his confronting authorities protecting themselves from ideas, desires, and people that frightened them. Once explosive in candidly presenting gay life, the novel had lost its subversive upending of sexual mores only to gain significance in the larger political sphere. The students saw the midcentury gay men as wrestling for their true, freeborn selves as a proxy for their current fight. Baldwin's American protagonist divulged the hidden face of their vexed identity. Like blacks and gays, the young people felt personal relations to be intolerably threatened by the culture. It was dangerous for them to be in love and to be themselves. They did not want to be at the mercy of the hegemonic consumerism (that's their phrase) telling them whom and how to love, who and what to be.

For Baldwin the freedom to love was a matter of life and death. *Giovanni's Room* stressed Baldwin's argument by upping the ante to murder and capital punishment. It was the era when feelings of sexual humiliation ran high. I explained the historical circumstances of class and nationality causing sexual dread in the 1950s. My response roused further questions, and so I spoke personally. "As a gay man who lived through post–World War II homophobia, I can vouch for the accuracy of the systemized terror menacing human relations in Baldwin's novel." The American internalizes the sexual politics of the era, which were coercive even in broadminded Paris (about sex for elites but not with residence permits for an alien bartender), where the love affair self-destructs. The hero rationalizes betraying his lover as the way to survive in a repressive, classist society. Having deserted his Italian partner to the shadow of the guillotine, the American enters of his own free will the status of political servitude.

A young woman eager to understand the struggle portrayed in *Giovanni's Room* asked for more details about being gay in 1950s. How

bad was it? Her bafflement merited truthfulness. It is always dangerous to love; safety in those days, I said, required persistent disguise
and constant invisibility. Clandestine relations necessitated coded language. To hear the self-mockery that passes for camaraderie and to
glimpse the denigrating effects of surrendering to fear, I recommended
Mart Crowley's play about a birthday celebration in *The Boys in the
Band*, now canonical but unnerving when it was produced in 1970.
The play honestly captures the subculture of campy men beating up
on themselves for being gay. As in the society they mock, the characters ridicule others for what they cannot accept in themselves. Some
birthday party! When I added that Mart Crowley and I were undergraduates together, another student asked, "Are you in the play?" I
wasn't. But I was in the fray of queer life Crowley depicted. And thanks
to the students I now was breathing the freer air of intellectual liberty
that they engendered.

The students were teaching me how to teach them, how we free
one another with honesty, just the way Frank and Nellie were showing
me how to love more openly. Being gay was crucial for both develop-
ments. My deepening investment in the classroom converted teaching
into a passionate conversation. Crossing the lines of discipline, generation, and belief brought back youthful strengths of personal engagement. The context of our discussion expanded. Soon Karl Barth joined
Toni Morrison at the table; Martin Buber, Thomas Merton, Dorothy
Day, and *The Tibetan Book of the Dead* accompanied Walker Percy,
Thomas Pynchon, and Don DeLillo.

The passion I felt with Frank and Nellie accomplished a parallel expansion in my scholarship. When I began to write, I adhered to the New
Critical approach of my generation that focused on close textual reading and well-wrought structures in literature. Politics and religion were
regarded as irrelevant to airtight aesthetic entities. My first book, *Music
in Willa Cather's Fiction*, published in 1967, traced musical allusions
and performances in Cather's writing to show how the human voice,
when lifted into song, expressed interior struggles that shaped the patterns of Cather's art. *Vonnegut: A Preface to His Novels* (1976) aimed

for a comparable exegesis of Kurt Vonnegut's writing. While my life-long interest in spirituality informed both studies, faith was secondary to the goal of stimulating interest in Cather and Vonnegut as a means for further scholarly investigation.

Flannery O'Connor brought the concern for faith to a position of artistic and moral determination in my research. Until the announcement that O'Connor was coming to speak in 1962 at Notre Dame, she was to me just a name. Actually, I had assumed Flannery was a southern male name. In preparation for her lecture, I read her stories in *A Good Man Is Hard to Find* (1955) and taught them to sophomores. Her writing hit me with a bolt of fresh energy. O'Connor puts abstract theology back on its tracks to propel the drama of sin and salvation into blood-spattered lonesome gullies and roads of Georgia and Tennessee that abut the stink and sweat of Golgotha. Then her laserlike prose slices through layers of social coverings and shibboleths to probe the radical need for belief beneath the nihilism of everyday modern life. A spree killer, a child suicide, and numerous tricksters conning various deceits are looking for God and don't know that they are. Driven by guilt and loneliness, the characters slash their way with fist and tongue through southern hinterlands.

Against all odds and intentions, violence opens the way for God to enter these shattered lives. With confrontational originality O'Connor shows how divinity with unaccountable tenderness intervenes amid bloodshed. Her characters stare at the reader amazed from the page, vulnerable to the narrator's raptor-eyed scrutiny. Their faces lay bare torpor, privation, and radiance. O'Connor telescopes Sophoclean grandeur into American dark ravines. Already perplexing, the narratives move ever more deeply in mystery with God's accommodation to humankind, especially in the modern condition of unbelief. The action does so by inverting the usual cozy relation of reader to text into the modern stance of interrogated and interrogator. As in scripture, nothing is idealized in O'Connor's short stories and novels. And all of the exposed gore comes to us from a southern woman who favors gentility and social convention.

This is a writer I needed to pursue. This is a God I needed to know about. O'Connor aligns the coordinates of literature and belief to the magnetic north of my work and life. Like her master-teacher Dante, O'Connor thinks of literature as theology and in her nonfiction writing reads theology as literature.

Tom Stritch, the colleague who invited O'Connor to Notre Dame, introduced her to me. She was cordial and proper and summarily went her busy way on aluminum crutches and left me in the wake of her visit. For years I taught O'Connor's stories and circled their hidden force. The glacial impact of her imagination rumbled in me without acquiring clear shape. Little by little a prophetic voice emerged. The disturber of the peace from middle Georgia acquired the shattering accent of Elijah, the "troubler of Israel." Then O'Connor's letters came out in *The Habit of Being* in 1979 to reveal a gift of sympathy that complicated my response still more. In her correspondence she is a modest, ambitious writer of quiet dignity with a respect for her gift as sacred. The fiction that initially hit me as explosion moderated into prayer with the felt intimacy one expects from poetry. The supernatural pervaded the everyday. Steeped in holiness, her fiction and letters stabbed me in the heart.

I wasn't ready for O'Connor. I wanted to write about O'Connor and couldn't. I needed to live more, and to live closer to the spiritual struggle of others. HIV and Nellie brought me further into myself. My mother's wracked body resonated to the physical grotesques through which O'Connor channels divine grace. For fourteen years O'Connor suffered the ravages of lupus, from which she died at the age of thirty-nine; and she saw that the body was good. But how did she know that? I too wanted to call the body good. I believed that God meant us to love our physical life.

With Nellie and Frank at my side, I began writing about O'Connor. I took the pleasure of turning to her short stories and novels to form an impression of their power while seeking to answer such questions as necessarily arise from divine favor. The word *grace* fills O'Connor's letters. *Love* is rarely used, and yet love struck me as the foundation of her art and faith. To understand O'Connor's treatment of love, I turned to biblical and theological sources for precedents. They brought me back to the young female prophet in O'Connor's second novel, *The*

Violent Bear It Away. "Love," the crippled evangelist of twelve proclaims, "cuts like the winter wind and the will of God is plain as the winter."

These stern words made sense to me. Love for O'Connor is the sword that cuts away all that is not divine is in. Crucially, she wrote from inside love's pain and release through faith. The result is an art that conceals art to the degree that the writer disappears into the moment uniting God and humankind. I set out to explore that dimension of O'Connor's genius. While caring for Nellie and feeling her love piercing my heart, I wrote *Flannery O'Connor and the Mystery of Love.* The study came out in 1989, three years after Nellie died, during the onset of Marie's chronic illness, and during the maturing of my partnership with Frank.

When we value people, we never weary of knowing them better. O'Connor's ruthless honesty disarmed me. O'Connor, in company with Frank and the dying women, has that ceaseless appeal for me. I had invested my heart in O'Connor's work. There was more to this convergence. A passing comment in one of O'Connor's letters got me going again. "Those desert fathers," O'Connor wrote to a friend, "interest me very much." Whoever these figures were (there were women too), they had to be very wise to command O'Connor's moral attention. The legendary ascetics of late antiquity had also been whispering to me through the writings of Thomas Merton and other spiritual masters. I read and wondered about the lives and sayings of these bizarre renouncers. They did not seek to live in the eyes and mind of the world. Instead, they embraced aloneness as the condition for seeking God. The hermits persevered in barrenness by heeding a simple rule: "Be solitary, be silent, be at peace." The directive sent me back to the founding conditions of faith in which Frank, dying women, and I lived. We were solitaries united in the effort to draw close to God. In 2000, our collective desert experience flowered into *Flannery O'Connor, Hermit Novelist.* The lives we were saving were our own.

Thanks to O'Connor, the desert mothers and fathers afforded insights into the suffering that AIDS was causing. It was warfare, it truly was, within and from without. The plague of darkness was another satanic outbreak. The evil impact on persons with AIDS was inescapable. AIDS pulled me into its pandemonium of scapegoating and misery. The virus took an immense toll on the communal and individual spirit.

Besides the medical front, there was the cultural line of battle. As usual, the way in which society deals with disease exposes deep-rooted truths about us all. Religious vigilantism seized the day. Our blame culture quickly pronounced the disease to be a judgment on a reckless and dissolute sexual minority. The local Taliban with collective ferocity revved up for attack. Infection marked sufferers as detested outcasts. A few of those living with HIV howled against the stigma; many bore disgrace quietly; all groaned. Exposure to harsh rebuke drove those with HIV into a loneliness that sharpened their heavy physical burdens. Shame for some sufferers became a basis for identity, with the disastrous consequences that came from needing to hide. In this state of internalized cultural scorn, the soul had to feel without outer guidance or inner support. HIV seemed like a deathblow to self-worth.

There is nothing like grief to stimulate the desire for consolation by seeking meaning in suffering. Illness seemed everywhere. There were, undeniably, differences between Nellie's dementia and infection with HIV; but for me there was a primal connection. Nellie's aloneness in losing a sense of herself helped me recognize the loss and mortification experienced by those living with HIV. Certainly, I did not encounter in Cedar Grove the swift currents of sexually transmitted diseases pouring through the streets and apartments of New York, but the tides of mortal danger were not far away. Disease and the pain it wreaked were part of the natural scheme of things. All things are God's. AIDS and dust too.

Looking at the HIV desert through a lens of desert spirituality allowed me to muddle through the daily bewilderments on both sides of the Hudson. Far from evading the stench and sweat of the disease, I sought a way to sweep the human body's foulest discharges and monstrous deformities up into the design of providence. Seen through the suffering and disorientation from one's true identity caused by HIV, I felt that God had sent us to the wilderness. At the same time, I trusted that this modern desert offered another exodus. But who or what would lead the departure?

Admittedly, the contemporary passage hardly felt like a way out of bondage so much as it appeared to be bands of people being thrown into a dark abyss. Clusters of gay roommates, some of them five and six in all, died of AIDS. At one point, there was a club called "90–9," in which 90 percent died within nine months of diagnosis. Membership in this group qualified one as marks to insurance predators who offered life settlements that paid pennies on the dollar of policies. Insurance companies made a meal of people with AIDS. The scams turned quick profits for those battening on the withering bodies of the young. Instead of moving toward the Promised Land, the journey seemed to end in the G-9 AIDS ward of Roosevelt Hospital. To walk down the hallway of St. Vincent's Hospital was to see the names of neighbors on room doors. It was a case of terminal cases. And yet, hope, as in the Exodus, was also a way of looking at the disaster.

After all, the creator of life was always making things new, unexpectedly new, disease included. HIV might occasion a new exodus with its own trial and its own fruitful period of deliverance. Might signs of human tenderness flourish anew to move the maker of all things? Could the crippled and the weak recover enough strength to prepare for the departure? Where will support come from? In the old exodus, the Lord carried the bedraggled group on his wings and was the guide. Can the water and blood gushing from the sides of the young, dying gay men refresh the people? Have the wounded the energy to raise their eyes to the source of life?

In the Book of Exodus, God brought the wanderers to the desert to speak to them and to reclaim their love. Some turned a deaf ear to the call. As the human was in scripture, so humankind was in the HIV desert. Betrayal was at the ready. Some families disowned their sons out of shame. Some men abandoned their infected partners in anger over infidelity mixed with outright fear of induction into the 90–9 club. For a stable partnership in which one person was positive, there was another kind of painful forsaking. They loved each other and couldn't make love unreservedly; even sex was Russian roulette. And there was the inevitable victimizing in American religious politics of the exposed sick by the hard Christian right who insisted that HIV was divine retribution for contaminating society. By the light of murderous hatred, the vile bodies of gay people deserved final destruction.

In defiance of all this institutionalized enmity, countless gay men responded to the call for compassion. Their work needed no exalted language to account for its religious value. What they did was all the more sacred because it was not undertaken for reward or show. They cooked, bathed, and dressed sick friends and strangers. Gay lawyers wrote wills for the dying. At St. Joseph's Church on Sixth Avenue a prayer group frequently collected money to pay for medication for those who lacked insurance. Such positive action signaled a collective turning of the heart away from bars, baths, and self-concern to the medical and legal protection of others. *Conversion* strikes me as the right word for this cultural shift among gay men. Like all deep transformations, this turning of the heart in full seriousness to serve others was altering gay identity.

Little by improbable little, gay people and friends responded. No slogans; no banners; no marches. Before a media mogul bought and furnished an official building for the Gay Men's Health Crisis in Chelsea with state-of-the-art equipment, there was a set of tiny rooms above a Chase Bank branch on Sheridan Square, operated by a ragtag, unpaid staff. Here an impromptu hotline opened for the latest information about AIDS or to let worried callers know that someone was listening to them. Volunteers and social workers provided crisis counseling, legal representation, the buddy system, and whatever medical help they could before the virus was found and the test for it was developed. Clients came to this warren as though entering a speakeasy. One rang a bell, spoke into the intercom, went through the buzzed door, and walked up two flights to a small oasis of support.

Though the *New York Times* did not include the term *gay* in its style guide until 1985, the gay rights movement was coming of age. The revolution of sexual freedom gave way to the counterrevolution of ethical responsibility. By necessity, people who could not find the services available in mainstream society learned to care for one another. Angels, as

Tony Kushner's play influentially put it, were broadcasting messages in America. The misshapen bodies of the messengers were the message.

Those dispatches struck home. Three young men (not counting the young man who walked the dog for our next-door neighbor) on the floor of our apartment building on Jane Street died of complications of the disease. The nearest to us was Allen. Sweet Allen, as Frank called our fit thirty-something neighbor and friend across the hall in 3S. Fit and elegant, he was an executive at a high-end travel agency. After years of cycling around Provence and swimming Amalfi beaches, Allen spent his final year struggling to go four blocks by taxi to St. Vincent's Hospital for treatment. Surgery for melanoma mangled his legs. When he couldn't walk across the hall for dinner in our apartment, Frank and I brought the food to him, along with his favorite Nestlé's Raisinettes. The chocolate-covered treats were morsels of affliction.

Allen's luxurious international expanse of four-star hotels shrank to a 400-square-foot studio apartment and eventually shriveled to a bed in an AIDS ward at St. Vincent's Hospital on West 12th Street. The fine French sauces he savored would have been pointless. He could no longer eat because a fungus clogged his mouth, throat, and arteries. Drinking, even breathing, caused pain. Finally, at Allen's request, the physicians stopped all medications. Newly empowered, Allen looked forward to death as a relief from decrepitude and dying. After Allen died, his two sisters held a service at Redden's Funeral Home on West 14th Street, an old blue-collar funeral service that handled the bodies of people with HIV when other funeral places wouldn't. Fear of the unknown was that intense. HIV was defilement. Flouting professional reluctance, Redden's served as the Joseph of Arimathea of our day. Piety was risky; decency was private. Nothing was safe. Grief came to wear a hangdog look. Divine intervention seemed light-years away.

At the weekday 5:30 evening Mass at St. Joseph's Church, there were invariably emaciated men in their mid-twenties to early forties. Clothes drooped on these ancient boys. Pustules pitted the withered flesh of several. One man scarcely more than thirty had a bulbous red nose with blisters from a disease called sporotrichosis, which, I learned, afflicts coal miners. Several had purple blotches of Kaposi's sarcomas on their arms and faces. Some sported baseball caps to keep facial lesions shaded out of clear sight of onlookers. Each had a favorite hat that he habitually wore. Of the various head coverings, the red hat with a B decorated in blue and white for the Red Sox stuck out. The wearer was boyish. I kept a maternal eye out for the out-of-town fan. A few men used makeup to screen darkened facial spots.

But nothing they put on or wore covered the bones of suffering or muted the sound of sickness. Coughs from the pews punctuated the words of God from the altar. Dry, muffled, or cackling, these involuntary spurts were anticipated and so distinctive that without looking around I could identify by the pitch and vibration who among the 5:30 regulars and irregulars had arrived for the late afternoon Mass. Those who did make it brought little more than spirit and gumption to the Lord's Table.

Such perseverance reminded me of the unpredictable and contradictory power that suffering exerts. Anguish, like abject poverty, does not necessarily unite us with God. Living in wrack and ruin has the potential to separate us from him. The courage of these persons with AIDS threw me back on my failings before sickness and life, which is to say, before God. I was grateful that I did not have AIDS—yet—because I would probably not be able to take it. AIDS did, in fact, drive a handful of the afflicted to despair. Approval of the HIV test in 1985 sharpened anxiety. Many men who didn't get tested assumed that they were going to die, and did. Our internist, for one, planned in what emergency room, with whom attending, and how he would die.

Though the Catholic church had not been a mother to her gay children, some came anyway. I thought of this cadre as Isaiah's "distant peoples" in the second Servant Song whose return signals achievable restoration. The group brought life back into a church that left them for dead. It would be their act of spiritual defiance. Their presence at the 5:30 Mass displayed the spectrum of AIDS from halting gait and blemishes to emaciation. Because death was inevitable and imminent, every stage for me was full-blown suffering. The relentless spectacle of HIV was not making people realize that religion was helpless and the world was ugly but had caused them to appreciate the sheer desperate tenacity of the love of life in these stricken men.

And so the pockmarked congregants lined up for sustenance, more life. What was stirring about their approach was how for all the differences in age and degree of disfigurement, the men walked without individual emphasis as universal petition to the Lord. The vitality of their appeal stood out in sharp relief against the lifeless Christianity that vilified their gayness. Not from the dead spirit of clerical bureaucrats but from these famished bodies the Eucharist rises. And at weekday liturgy divine goodness renews itself daily at the table God spread in the desert.

The procession down the aisle seeking nourishment—for the food and drink that feed the bond of fellowship—called to mind the historic Seder and re-created that ancient foreboding in the way we live now. AIDS, for me, was our passion. Its agony thrust gay life into the vortex of biblical and twentieth-century history. It took AIDS to vault homosexuality out of a subculture and into national debate. To get a handle on the disease the *New York Times*, the Gray Lady of print journalism in charge of the current record, began on the inside pages to cite sexual practices implicated in the virus. Explicit language also entered governmental debate that in the past hardly acknowledged the epidemic.

This previously censored truthfulness came to rest in rows of church benches for all to bear gayness in mind as part of providential history. In a sense, this is what the liturgy is all about for me: divine sacrifice correcting human vision to reveal the full humanness of pariahs as potential bearers of grace. Hope needs such a story. The supper's narrative from word to bread directs us to the cross of Jesus, the sign of a divine curse that is the instrument of redemption. By remanding us to Calvary, the liturgy destigmatizes AIDS. The church should follow its own sign, stop making sport of gay people, and remove its mark of infamy on homosexuals.

The gospel reading and prayers leading to the sacrifice on the altar changed how I saw the human body. At the liturgy, persons with HIV twisted with disease were not seen as the reviled carriers of plague rejected by society. Bodies that were hosts for infections sought the host of sacred healing. Their return to the home that spurned them showed that the divine spirit was far beyond any barrier of separation that humans erected for themselves. The love that dare not say its name, much less demand marriage equality, howled out from its heart with what voice it had left to reclaim its place in God's plan. Worship modeled a church and society to which I felt I could belong.

The gathering of these persons with HIV put before me, as did no other public situation or ceremony, the way Christian liturgy can establish and recover when severed the relation between humankind and God. These devastated young men were doing in free obedience what they believed they had to do. Duty, however, came not from law decreed from the top down. It rose out of the bodily need and interior disposition each had of the creator upon whom they, all, utterly depended. These gay men came for help but did not beg for it. Their dignity reconfigured in recent conditions John's passion narrative in which Jesus moves toward the cross with majesty.

The touchable ravages of HIV called upon the history of God's work commemorated in the worship to make divine activity tangible in their lives. The past of merciful intervention from generation to generation in fidelity to divine covenant permits one to hope for sacred aid. Readiness to help in Hebrew scriptures mainly means to "be motherly." Mercy made the Mass authentic. *Only say the word and we shall be healed.*

The Psalms in particular confirm that expectation with the deeds of God animating the psalmists' personal lives. In these ancient hymns the prayers of the broken are immense. And they were present at St. Joseph's Church on Sixth Avenue. Disfigured seekers encircled us at the weekday liturgy. I could not help but have faith in the prayer of the stigmatized. Dorothy Day, in the way she lived and how she wrote, was a living reminder of the dispensation of the poor and broken. Of all the great reversals that scripture promises, none is more compelling than the way in which social disrepute and spiritual humility dispose one to the divine call and presence. The bodies of these persons with AIDS were keepers of faith. They knew what to do with their suffering. Somewhere in their trust there was God's zealous care. But where? In our care for one another, there and nowhere else?

One regular parishioner's mortal embattlement condensed the lessons I was receiving about the human body. He stood tall with a cane supporting him. He neither wore a hat nor used cosmetics to cover his malignant tumors. Such complete confidence in his skin inscribed with scarlet marks expressed a quiet and intractable dignity. He had faith in his body. He was not ashamed of his gift from God, his own skin, which is something to think about. It was as though this young man was bringing each day in slow motion his entire person of ensouled flesh to the final judgment for the anticipated life of his resurrected body. One day he no longer showed up at the 5:30 liturgy.

It was like that. HIV was a disease of disappearance. After people were out of sight, the heart brought them back to table fellowship as privileged gifts with the bread and wine. There was no end of offerings.

One morning, the coffin of a friend from the past, Bob, was before the altar at St. Joseph's. The church was filled with many of his friends from AA. This support group provided the communal ties that Bob first sought with his former Benedictine brothers. Bob and I were friends and housemates back in the early 1960s at Notre Dame, where we started our teaching careers. When a job in philosophy opened in New York, Bob at the top of his game gave up tenure at Notre Dame to start a new life in New York with a man he met here. "Love life" was the phrase Bob used to explain his move east. He used *love* as both imperative and adjective. After the liturgy at St. Joseph's, Bob was buried in Oregon, where he grew up. He made it home. Getting home summed up the drinking, the love-seeking, and soul-seeking that amounted to God-seeking. *My peace I give you.*

After the liturgy of Christian burial for Bob, my tears were never the same. In this season of death, a communal human flourishing came to surround persons living with and dying of HIV. There arose a sense of the goodness of human life in its most dire, despised state. Their bodies belonged not to those who loathed them, or to those who mourned them, but to the one who created them and sanctified their seeking. Gay men were seeking. They sought pleasure and love and human connections. They sought the fullness of life. Nothing was more basic. Nothing was more vexed and dangerous. We were with HIV/AIDS, I felt, back to where Augustine in his *Confessions* took a radical turn toward God. When he arrived in Carthage as a young man bucking with sexual urges, he found himself in "a hissing cauldron of lust." Not one to follow the "safe path without pitfalls" of his physical desires, Augustine immersed himself in the risky sexual churn.

The lustful adventure was as edifying as it was incomplete in answering Augustine's hunger for love. There are readers who find that conversion brought Augustine to hate flesh. I read him differently. Far from disparaging his sexual relations, he saw them as a condition that led him to God, the need for whom was intertwined with his sexuality. Erotic desire coincided with spiritual yearning. Both drives were for life, more life. If God met Augustine through the most intimate contacts of his life, God could meet us in the metropolis of naked lust that was New York. Flesh was the condition of hope. If we were to stumble upon him in the stark mystery of what we were confronting, the bodies of gay men that seemed so distant from the divine had to be the sites of our encounter with God.

AIDS was forcing us to cross the threshold of fear into the dark of God's presence, a presence that was part of everydayness. The entrance opened not through dogmatic Christianity. Disincarnate statements gave no understanding and therefore no compassion for suffering. For me to grasp the vocabulary of death and redemption, the words had to be written in torn ligaments and blocked arteries. The material body had to show the way to the return to life we call resurrection. I sensed the collective hope at the liturgy. During the worship the desperate struggle of people with AIDS to make themselves whole came to the surface with unabashed immediacy and moral intensity. They, we, all were there under the shadow and promise cast by the slain body on the crossbeam.

We will always have the liturgy, and there will always be New York; but I have never felt the same about both after attending the 5:30 Mass at St. Joseph's during the AIDS pandemic. Neither worship nor the city gave rest. Their continuance was not the permanence I needed.

One of Flannery O'Connor's most inspired comments about faith comes to us, as does so much of her wisdom, in the spontaneity of a letter responding to a friend's religious questioning about the divine nature. "I measure God," O'Connor wrote in February 1961, "by everything that I am not." Her theology of negation describes what was going on in New Jersey. God was hunting me down in the suburb of illness so that I could plumb the depth of my deficiencies. There in New Jersey the mind, my mother's and mine, strained to keep itself intact. The HIV epidemic brought me home to Nellie across the Hudson in a prayerful way. I didn't know my HIV status and was too afraid to be tested. And so I played the coward's game of asking God that I live long enough during the HIV catastrophe to care for Nellie until she died. Caring for Nellie helped me cope with terror. Those who remained alive fell into that strange category of fortune—the good luck that was unnecessary had not unspeakable bad fortune preceded it.

I was caught between a rock and an AIDS place. With death so close to Manhattan life, going to Nellie in woodsy Cedar Grove afforded a breathing space. Young gay men dying and aged senile mother equally pounded my heart, but next to the sorrow evoked by friends with HIV, the crush experienced from Nellie felt like joy. Caregiving was a serious need. It conserved my sanity.

Being with Nellie could be peaceful until it was chaos. Then she drove me nuts. Every so often, after stretches of stasis, her brain went haywire. The first time her neurotransmitters and muscles went out of control lasted an interminable half-hour. While sitting in her chair, Nellie's body burst into repetitive up-and-down motions bending to tie laces on shoes that she no longer wore. Spastic commotion kept coming and going. Her nervous system acted like an organ coupled to her body. I was helpless before these contractions, and I was scared that her brain's sudden realignments would never cease. Maybe I could go upstairs to my old bedroom and cry, but tears weren't in me. Nor was a primal scream or throwing a chair against the wall. What was going on in Nellie's mind? Is this what parents of an autistic child go through day after day? An old woman dies, but a child lives many years. I couldn't budge from her side.

There was no telling what turn her neural pathways would take next. A number of times when we sat in the back yard, her optic nerves didn't communicate the command to close her eyelids and block the sun hitting her eyes. Then her arms thrashed wildly to shake away the blinding light. Total exhaustion, not anything I did, stopped her. Besides grappling with my demons of helplessness, I was battling biology. Trying to tamp down the unruly eruptions that go with dementia was futile.

Paradoxically, true satisfaction came in those periods of annoyance by finding a calm place in myself from which I might see Nellie's uncontrolled flailing not as making demands on me but as what they did for her. The gyrations relieved her. Her muscles had a memory of their own yet strangely connected to her central nervous system. Whatever she had to convey or get rid of was expressed in her arms and hands. Intermittently, Nellie threaded phantom needles that she used years earlier when she sewed clothes for herself and her children. On occasion she mended in pantomime; if there was no fabric, there was her restiveness to patch up. Perhaps she was repairing connections with the outer world by stitching together a sock for my father, or putting finishing touches on the new dress she was making for her first-born daughter's return home from the hospital that never happened. Whatever Nellie was doing, she and I were better off when I ceased judging her behavior by conventional measures. I was learning a new interpretive framework, one founded in tolerance of the unexpected.

Nellie's synapses and motor neurons simply did what tangled nerve cells do. Had I patience, I could have seen that life, which is to say God, was delivering me from myself by taking the matter out of my hands. If I had just let anxiety go, I could have seen that because Nellie's erratic movements caused no harm, they troubled no one and possibly gave her a numbing ease.

In time, the episodes went unnoticed. All I had to do was to stand by Nellie. Put on her slippers, wipe coatings from her crusty eyelids with a warm face cloth, wash the urine-stained pillow she sat on in the living room, and coax her to eat a stewed prune. These small successes made the day. Even the worthless felt important. Reason and talk were beside the point. So was my exasperation. I had, like stricken Nellie, to go through my own nervous spasms to find emotional quiet. Complex and little-known laws were governing changes in me as well.

I spent much of the day with Nellie bent over her body either in her bed, at kitchen table, in the living room chair, and back in bed. My hands smelled of soap and lotion. I was useful.

It was the silence with Nellie that led the way through our obscure relationship. Unmediated by sound, her presence spatially portrayed her life set within the final artifacts of her life. Enclosed by light brown walls and faded green carpet, she slumped like a rag doll in her beige living room chair. She, who had murmured *sogni d'oro*, golden dreams, as she tucked me into bed as a child, had whistled while she cleaned the house, and had hummed while dusting and sewing, was now mute. Those tuneful supplements to her loneliness petered out. Our past, the present, and Nellie's future were unspoken.

The stillness that was Nellie brought me to wonder if there was inner groaning and what story unfolded in the fading brain at the back of her closed eyes. Behind the veil of obvious physical decay was the whole inscrutable mystery of her life: her first five years as a child in the rugged Abruzzo Mountains, her relations with her reclusive mother, her other children, with her husband, with her sisters, prejudices, dreams, the web of influences in which dying entangled her. My mother's past came back to me in bits and pieces, each time reshaped by the moment of my remembering, or of imagining that is integral to memory.

I came to welcome the stillness Nellie embodied. Without recalling the time or the reason, I found myself breaking a lifelong habit of listening to classical music as an accompaniment to whatever I was doing. Saturday afternoons with Nellie passed without my tuning in WQXR for the Metropolitan Opera broadcasts. I forgot what Nellie's voice sounded like; I used my voice less. Nellie was the nearest person to what is understandable and lovable. And of course she was always a mystery. All of this came if I emptied my ears of wanting to hear her wishing me "golden dreams" again. Then, by anticipating silence, I found in that silence whatever there was to hear.

As I drew near to Nellie's dying, I learned that there was no other way to deal with her mounting medical problems other than with humility. I felt well off when I accepted our shared inner helplessness. If

I responded from a sense of poverty, everything came as a gift. By the light of gratitude, Nellie's silence was not a symptom of her disease but a ray of inner tranquility brightening my disquiet. Her accepting help—no easy thing to do—was a grace gift to me. Trifles counted. If she smiled, the expression beamed pleasure into me. Our poverty was a window open on a kind of love that offered no rewards other than enduring the ache of imminent loss.

And so I trudged the way to that remained unknown. But I had Frank at my side. His physical closeness supported the teaching in Nellie's sick body and mind. Watching Nellie's decline showed me that I couldn't make it alone. No one could. I was suffering from delusions of adequacy. Frank was at hand to rebuild the inherently flawed temple of self-worth. His help with my mother consecrated our partnership. Friendship directed toward others is faith.

Because Nellie and Marie had no social model for relating to Frank and me as lovers, their letting us help them served as favorable reception. Both his family, which was notably traditionalist, and mine were left to deal with us as individual persons. In that way, their hearts received us. Frank's parents welcomed my visits with emotional warmth and great food. Nellie and Marie expected that Frank and I would sleep upstairs together in my old bedroom.

As I said, Nellie's infirmity was a school for trust. Her total dependence taught me to respond to Frank in a way that I otherwise might not have learned. By his nature, Frank fell into helping Marie to help Nellie. He was genetically wired for family. He shopped, brought prepared meals from his mother, kept Marie's car in shape, resurfaced the driveway, repaired the back fence, and planted new trees and tulips. He hugged us all, all the time. Frank's functional loyalty cut a path through the social hostility surrounding us. The straitlaced Cedar Grove neighbors waved to him as he pulled up into the driveway. With Frank I felt that my being dependent was a grace, a grace I aspired to.

The circle of Nellie's frailty, if strewn with ashes, was warm with life's embers. Every silence and gesture, including the frustrating motions between us, lived in these smoldering remains as nowhere else. One thinks that the woman who gives one birth and raises one through early years serves her nurturing purposes and then goes on to live out her own life. Like so much else in Nellie's life, she was an exception to the maternal pattern. Nellie was a woman more for later times in my life than the first two decades. We came together again for the season of final harvest. Our eleventh-hour relationship tapped me into her family's tradition of sisterly service that decades of life in America had not worn away. This drawing on gentle female service occurred as I, Nellie's gay middle-aged son, grew first into her younger sister and then matured into being her mother. Nellie was the duty that was becoming my need.

The chores of mothering were a remedy for the incompleteness I have always felt in my soul. Nursing squared the diverse parts of my life. The scholar-teacher in me enjoyed being the domestic worker. Crossing gender lines to become my mother's mother taught me about the concealed strength of humility. Throughout her life, Nellie numbered among the unremarkable people who lived without honors and prestige. She was as ordinary as the loaf of five-cent pizza bread sold at the Violante Bakery down Fifteenth Avenue on 12th Street in Newark where she raised us.

At Nellie's physical peak, she was plain. She weighed about 125 pounds, stood just over 5 feet, had a pale complexion, and usually kept her hair combed into a bun. Even when she was dressed up for a wedding, the most fancy occasion, her clothes aspired to unassuming propriety. She had a slightly bow-legged walk that grounded her slight figure in confidence. Others did not seek Nellie out as interesting or sociable. Nor did she make friends easily. The world, you see, had no curiosity about the interior virtue that comes with accepting oneself as being one of many. Her way was to pass through the world as a bird sails through the air—heedless of attention, leaving no marks. That anonymity in living and dying interested me more than did my trendy neighbors in Greenwich Village who were supposedly accomplished or exciting or sexy.

Steeped in a culture prizing intelligence and prosperity, I was more attracted to the tenderness, poverty, and shadows of Nellie's final years. Nellie commanded even less notice than she had in previous decades. Her illnesses were ordinary and predictable for an old woman. Hers was a history seemingly without interest, a story almost lost in the mighty landscape of time. To the end, I understood that outsiders might not see anything special in her—in whom I was seeing no end of things. Or perhaps I should say in whom I saw how to prepare for the end of things.

At Nellie's shriveled feet with cramped toes from tight low-cost shoes when she was a girl lay another world, a poor one of riches. If just being with ailing Nellie bestowed such largesse, what would come from staying on as a witness to her last days and as her companion unto death?

Nellie, who made me feel special as a child, brought me in middle age to appreciate the consolations of ordinariness. Ambition was less enticing. I was tired of proving myself. I was weary of sticking out. I was no longer reluctant to be one of many. What was a great relief!

To idealize Nellie's final years is to distort her integrity by depriving her life of its hard, tattered truth. If Nellie's universe was hidden and quiet, her suffering was by no means lofty. Her losses were relentlessly mean and cruel. She was dying by inches. She shrank to the point of bone outlined under her skin. Nellie was the human condition in its state of dryness.

The aridity could drain my staying power. Fatigued annoyance took hold. My efforts to be hospitable frequently soured into hostility. No sooner did I change Nellie's diaper than she might soil it. At eighty pounds or so, she could be dead weight to lift. She hardly sipped milk. When she did, it sometimes dribbled on her clean shirt. I was easily irritated by her and annoyed with myself. As I was powerless before her deterioration, I battled petty things, such as untimely phone calls and weak coffee and dirty dishes in the sink. It was sometimes impossible to check edgy reactions to her natural bodily breakdowns.

Not only did resentment and a moody flatness frequently settle on me; this spiritual lowness disposed me to fear. Fear attracts demons. Fear of being alone, fear of being consumed, fear of silence, fear that there was no end to binding Nellie's wounds, and fear of death. I feared

aging into Nellie's dependence, as though even in a state of unawareness I would be aware of my abject reliance on others. On bad days,
fear spread out into a fatalistic sense of life running down like a clock,
and caring for my mother was killing time. Acts of service became a
war of nerves.

Irresolvable emotions held me captive because I sought resolutions.
Attending Nellie to her death conferred no laurels to rest on. Nor were
there places to take it easy along the way. There was no end in sight. I
feared her death at the same time that I hoped that she would die
without pain, and quickly. Certainly she would die without blame.
Then, seeing the end in view for Nellie put the day of my death before
me.

My desire to do what was right for Nellie was not a matter of a
single will but many wills conflicting in me. I still rebelled against the
institution of the family with its tyranny imposed under the name of
blood or love. Nevertheless, exterior compliance as a mothering son
somehow, gradually and unexpectedly, became a compliance of the
heart. I settled for the stamina to stand by Nellie day by day. I was not
looking to religion as a good feeling or a sense of association but as a
constant purpose. Seeking without finding was believing.

Nellie may have had nothing to do with God or institutionalized religion, but God had something to do with her. The emotions that belong
to religion—terror, consolation, elation—were felt with Nellie. In her
ailing years, she imprinted a sentiment of faith in her gay son who also
had turned his back on the church. Beneath the spiritual and mental
humiliations brought by dementia, Nellie endured the grace to surrender to what was in store for her. The body of my unbelieving mother
was where a force beyond every force was acting. Holiness, contrary
to all conventional expectation, was not a matter of perfection and
righteousness, or even religion with its pious categories detached from
the failure and stink of the way we live. What genuine trust that did
evolve between Nellie and me was in the physical. That's where God
began to be.

Basic bodily rituals were a divine office for me. Lauds was seeing
Nellie smile when I got her out of bed; Matins was bathing her and

the breaking fast over stewed prunes and Cheerios; Vespers came with a peaceful recollection after supper; Compline, my favorite liturgical hour, completed the day with my maternal hug to my mother. Each of the hours carried us along, as we were not rushing to get anywhere else. Intervals were part of a whole cycle. Similar to the recitation of Psalms and readings, the round of daily bread and daily sadness with Nellie consecrated ordinary time. The inner life of Nellie's shrinking world opened out to a self-styled monastic life.

Sometimes nothing ever happened, and I liked it that way. Nellie and I mostly spent a good part of the day in a familiar silence. Nellie fixed in her chair, I stationary at the end of the table. Each sat like the pianist in John Cage's silent piece of music that lasts for four minutes and thirty-three seconds without a note being played at the keyboard. This silence chastened my soul. The flow and quiet pulsed with death. Instead of sound, there was a rhythm of the spirit that lost a lot and gained a subdued triumph in a resonance beyond time. The quiet duet bid us to listen closely so that we can feel what we cannot hear in each other's stilled voices. The moment's music arose not through notes but by way of an interior rhythm of loss and life, of love and failure, and all other contrasts in the harmony of life.

When Nellie was too weak to sit in the dining room chair next to where I sat reading and taking notes for class, she sat in the shiny champagne-colored upholstered chair near the table from which I could keep an eye on her. Despite several washings to remove the urine stains that traced the impression of Nellie's bony buttocks, the spotted imprint remained. The smudge marked the indelible duty to Nellie that I tried to wipe away, resisted, frequently resented, and in due course pressed to my breast.

7   Death and the Remainder of Life

Suffering, above all, suffering which has a strong element of physical pain, is a mystery of solitude, a country into which one penetrates all alone.

—*Interior Prayer*, Carthusian Novice Conferences

On an early September morning in 1985, something new developed in Nellie. The change showed up right after I carried Nellie from her bed to the bathroom to get us ready for the day. As usual, she was sitting naked on the toilet. As usual, I was feeding her crushed stewed prunes sprinkled with flax meal to prevent constipation. This time when she tried to swallow, sharp pain squashed an absent grin on her face. Tears coated her aching eyes. The mushy fruit would not go down. Some blockage was hurting her. Food must have been like stones caught in her throat.

I was stumped, again. Nellie had enjoyed eating small bits of food. I knew better than to force breakfast. Her body was my guide, the only compass to channel through her shadowed life of advanced dementia. I began mashing food and bought Gerber's pulverized pears and apples for variety. Nellie could barely manage baby food. She gradually lacked the muscular strength to propel food and liquid down to her stomach.

By the fall of 1985, approximately eighteen years after the early onset of symptoms, Nellie, now housebound for five or six years, was getting by without doctors. Mental disease, as I was slowly recognizing, is also a progressive affliction that destroys the body as it shuts down the brain. Her inability to swallow required that she receive medical attention. I called a physician friend for advice. He suggested that, while Nellie was still lying down in bed in the morning, I should cover her eyes with a cloth, gently hold her tongue down with a spoon, and look down her throat with a flashlight (thank you, Martin). I did that. Greenish stained-red swellings lined her gullet. Although I had never seen cancer before, I knew the disease when I saw it. Who knew how long the tumors had been growing there? Cancer insidiously can show no sign of malignancy until its late stage causes pain. In her quiet, long-suffering way, Nellie might have been living with the stony bulges for some time. Mental incapacity rendered her unable to report any difficulty.

An oncologist came to the house, confirmed my observation, and said that he would "have to do a section." Marie expressed no reaction, as if she hadn't heard or understood the doctor's judgment. I said to myself and to Nellie in our silent language, "Never." Enough was enough. The idea of invasive treatment, hospitalization, and dubious recovery from doubtful intervention to prolong life, if the options did extend life, distressed me.

Science was not the remedy. The physical toll of such treatment on Nellie would be significant. No surgery, nor would I permit a feeding tube to reduce her intact body to a receptacle for pharmaceutical nutrients. Cancer did more than change the condition of Nellie's life. It altered what I would do and rely on for Nellie's good. Her welfare became a matter of comfort and palliative care—and of my uncertain faith. The only life support I trusted was life itself. My faith was well placed. Several years later, I learned that esophageal cancer, like pancreatic cancer, was extremely difficult to treat, but Nellie's body presciently taught me what medicine could only subsequently confirm.

When I first found out about Nellie's cancer, I knew that I had to do something. Action, however, was not my first impulse. Anxiety, as usual, disabled me. I was stuck in a pattern of helplessness; Marie was caught in a history of denial. Marie was unwilling to admit that Nellie's death was near, and she refused to have any stranger come close to Nellie. My sister treated the physician who came as the enemy. For me he was a dispassionate messenger delivering the unwelcome facts of life. Such clarity was a form of freedom that soon mobilized me.

The surgeon was going by the books. I wanted to follow the heart and have a say in Nellie's dying and my survival through her dying. I knew hospice's work from their help with people suffering from AIDS. Because Marie lived with Nellie, she would have to agree to my proposal. After several days of trying to persuade Marie that we needed to take the next step in caring for Nellie, I called West Essex Hospice in Caldwell, about ten miles away. Hospice was new and scary to Marie. It meant that Marie would lose control, lose Nellie to intruders. Marie was right and understandably distraught. I, however, felt relief to have professionals help manage Nellie's dying. Nellie had lost her mind and had untreatable cancer. Surrender at this stage was part of the humbling experience of powerlessness. Spiritual work went with changing diapers. The job of caring for Nellie had involved muddling through my own error and lack of knowledge. Now that she was in the tightening grip of cancer, coping with my fear and ignorance was more critical.

Marie, Frank, and I needed to stick together for the troubles ahead. One of the looming tests of loyalty, Frank reminded me, would be Marie's heartache. Her emotional entanglement with Nellie called for solace, as did Nellie's misery from cancer. After all, unfamiliar persons were crossing the threshold into Marie's cherished privacy, upsetting her lifelong intimacy with Nellie. Anyone coming to help Marie was tantamount to someone breaking into her house. The new test of love for Frank and me would be to extend the maternal care of our dying mother to our grieving sister, who would soon be a late-life orphan.

The day after I called hospice, the nurse came. Her name escapes me, but not her vital service. She was direct and factual. First, we had to have a physician legally turn over decisions to a hospice nurse. Then, she explained how hospice worked. A nurse would visit every week to assess Nellie's care and come as needed should a medical problem arise. We should call hospice whenever we have questions. We agreed that nothing would be done to hasten Nellie's death; nothing would be done to extend her life. We would do what was needed to keep her comfortable and pain-free. When Nellie died, a nurse would come to pronounce her dead and call the undertaker. I was spared one crucial worry. Nellie was out of the clutches of invasive medical technology. No emergency room. No life-support machines. I trusted only life itself. She would die in her own way, in her own time, in her own bed at home. Marie and I signed the papers.

What lay ahead did not daunt this ready-for-anything nurse. How different this woman was from the procedure-dispensing male oncologist. By implication, we could follow this visiting nurse. Her strength, a distinctly female toughness forged in the trenches of terminal illness, was her unruffled consideration. Religion did not come up because it didn't have to. Doctrine was beside the point; trust meant caring action. Belief was all. The hospice woman was an envoy of healing. I had faith in her because there was not a trace of sentimentality or pontification in her voice and bearing. This stranger entered our lives as a friend of Nellie and an ally of life-in-death.

Our initial interview with hospice was in late October 1985. In early January 1986, Nellie and I were again in the bathroom, she on the toilet seat ready to have breakfast, I sitting on the edge of the bathtub. This time she couldn't swallow even prune juice without distress. Her facial muscles contracted into deep lines of pain that sank into root anguish. She let out a squeal. The cry pierced the air and went deeper into my flesh than any cut I ever experienced. Tears came to her eyes as if being pumped. Trying to be calm and focused on Nellie, as the hospice nurse was in every situation, I went out to meet the wail. "Nellie," I said quietly, "you won't have to eat any more." *Mai più, Nicolina.* I put down the soupspoon with the prune juice.

Because Nellie's hearing had been waning along with her mental condition, she probably had heard not with her ears the words of promise I made. Still, we spoke to each other. As I was learning to listen through her touches and breath on my skin, she was hearing speech through her eyes so foggy with cataracts. I could know what she understood only by what she did. Clearly, the vertical deep lines in my child-mother's face, which invariably suggested weariness, softened. The taut muscles of Nellie's face relaxed into a grotesque smile as big as a silent-movie actor's expression. Her lopsided mouth stopped twitching. She looked up from the toilet seat with her imbalanced watery eyes, one eye mourning, and the other grateful. This was the face of love, tangled, heart-smashing, lit up. If sickness robbed Nellie of cognitive powers, she still owned her emotions, which, she showed me, were always fresh.

Such contact was the pure oxygen of caring for Nellie. I read and heard our reciprocal triumph in Nellie's drenched eyes. Cancer was obstructing her esophagus. A lump stuck in my gullet. A strain I had not realized was wrenching us both. As she smiled, I was the one whose throat choked closed. Fluid pressed against my eye sockets. I wanted to carry the sadness of the moment with me to the end of time, for the world refracted through the tears of the moment, specifically the Nellie moment, was awash with the gospel's promise of sorrow overcome in progress all around me.

Nellie was scrawny in my arms, as skeletal as a prisoner seen in one of the Auschwitz photographs. With rickety bowlegs, she managed to stand on her own two feet by holding on with knobby hands to the towel rack as I cleaned her buttocks after a bowel movement. Her head and torso huddled easily in my chest. I was aware that the trust I felt from my child-mother may have been her accommodating dementia. Still, I felt faith between us. I don't know how direct contact with dying put me in the presence of joy, but it did.

The inward rest I sought in church I found in her arms. Seeking God at the liturgy gave way to the far truer seeking of God through the humble poverty of simple human caring. Nellie's physically trusting me dissolved the icy fear around my heart. The warmth in what was left of Nellie invited me to come in from the cold of lonely doubt about the Spirit whose lenient kindness of mercy met the hard truth of death in our coupled bodies.

If Nellie drew just a portion of the consolation from my upper body that I got from her rickety bones, then we were both in reliable hands. I felt the natural certainty that attends the nakedness of sheer visceral reliance. An unforced power bound us. Ordinary physical gladness gave me faith in the continuance of life. If God is at work in us, his touch must be here at the organic root of our being where the heart and mind are one.

Receiving the grace of trust necessitated my responding. I hugged Nellie, clutching her for the past—for the future. An *abbraccio clemente* united us in a mingling of succor, loss, and forgiveness, the very essence of maternity. Her body, the fragile token of our humanness, reassured me that flourishing of life was present all the way to the complete loss of it. And beyond. Old woman leanness and old woman tenacity were about more life. More life also meant more self-doubt. Even if I had the strength to obey God's will and care for Nellie, would I have the endurance to receive what God had promised?

All shall be well, Julian of Norwich assures us. No doubt she is right, but the ways in which providence makes things well can be burdensome. Such raw exposure to mercy that I felt with Nellie can make the blood run cold with retroactive forgiveness. The encounter had no prelude or sequel. The Nellie moment existed separately and outside of time. We were instantly alive to each other and parted in a flash. With this old woman's letting go of her spirit, I too gained a moment of liberty in the act of renouncing control of it. Abandonment gave me a sense of freedom. With no thought of myself, I smiled with her. Even Nellie seemed surprised by it all. Together our brightening faces expressed that we were alive to each other in the moment. The spirit does well in dotage. I placed my self with Nellie in the hands that sustain life when food did not.

The trust born of this unique closeness had, as I said, a terrible side. It caused me to be peculiarly sensitive to Nellie's suffering. The silent stirring of love made me feel that I could never love enough. Setbacks aplenty came afterward, but there was that surrender, close and complete, a life unto itself.

During her last weeks, Nellie was totally bedbound. Fine. Now I did not have to worry about finding her on the floor. No fractured bones. Good. For all her mental brokenness, Nellie in her eighty-six years never broke a bone. At long last, Marie consented to our hiring Christine, who came up from Newark to be with Nellie during the day while Marie was at school, working as a teacher and guidance counselor. Christine was indispensable. She, another strange woman and the first black person to set foot in the house, came to Nellie like a visitor from beyond with all the sensitive physical attention anyone could bring.

Nellie was manageable in bed. With her skin as thin as parchment, bedsores concerned me. When a lesion began, we kept the patch of red skin moist with Bacitracin ointment. Thanks to Christine's care and Marie's diligence, each wound healed, very slowly. Christine's gentle applications of Aveeno daily moisturizing lotion with oatmeal did the rest. One problem or another popped up. If not friable skin, then unproductive cough or swollen ankles. When asked by relatives how Nellie was, one could go through an organ recital. But why give physical details? She was sick. And on her own.

Nellie's final solitude had not changed her. It changed me. Aware of dwelling in the days of death—the moment of preparation and release—I stopped looking for things to worry about. Everything was new, unknown, and, with Nellie's end in sight, supportable.

Frank pitched in with greater regularity and finer affection. Hospice was ever more crucial. Besides their promptly answering telephone calls, the nurse's visits assured Marie and me that Nellie was comfortable. We were doing the right thing. That was no small reassurance to all four of us. Tylenol with codeine worked for the pain in Nellie's throat. That surprised me. Nellie could take in rich juices. I wondered if blood had ceased supplying the part of Nellie's brain that registered pain, and for that reason she no longer gave signs of experiencing pain. There was morphine on hand to assure the sleep of peace should pain set in. On several occasions the hospice nurse found that fluid was building in Nellie's lungs and legs. She recommended Lasix to relieve the strain of breathing. The diuretic worked, until it didn't.

Nellie on her deathbed, from her decrepitude, stared at me with a clear-eyed invitation not to disavow the human body but to love corruptible flesh as the material worthy of life and the divine spirit. With her flesh half-consumed, Nellie drew me toward the mystery of materiality. The relinquishing of life in Nellie's mind and devastatingly thin body forced me to try to love things precisely because they are subject to decay. Nellie's life and my death were one in this emptiness. I began to see the office of maternal care as a practicing for death. In this work as consoler and mediator the physical comes into contact with the spiritual. Death may be the mother of exaltation.

*   *   *

On Wednesday, January 22, 1986, the spring term of classes began. On Friday, January 24, Christine called me at Fordham to say that Nellie was "weaker," a euphemism for dying. I called Frank. We went to our apartment, got clothes, and drove to Cedar Grove, arriving around 3:30 that sunny afternoon. No ambulance with screaming sirens and flashing lights came to transport Nellie to a hospital's intensive-care unit. Nellie was asleep. Burdened only by life, she was in her own bed in the home she'd built for us.

Without an explanation or fanfare, Christine had vested Nellie for prayer. Nellie's squeaky-clean white hair was neatly combed back; her skin was recently washed and shone with lotion. Christine left the moment Frank and I arrived. Marie returned home from school around 4:00. The struggles of Nellie's disease-ridden body were near resolution. A stranger on earth was approaching her true abode in the totality of sacred geography.

Nellie's new course called for a formal acknowledgment, a simple observance, to mark the occasion with expectation and patience. But what form? Priests, like doctors, were the people Nellie least wanted around her. They embarrassed her. A forbearing female pastor as guide would have been right for the moment, but that was not to be. Although Nellie never expressed an interest in seeing a priest, I called St. Catherine of Siena Church, the Cedar Grove Catholic parish, to ask that a priest come. A young curate, whose name escapes me, came within the hour. The January day was cold, nearing sundown; but there was lingering brightness, the sharp kind of winter sunlight to bring in Nellie's new day.

The priest, Marie, Frank, and I stood around Nellie in her bed. He began with a greeting of peace. Our family never said grace before meals, and so this was the first time for spoken prayer in the Giannone home. I felt awkward about a ceremony with emotions prescribed in its words, but the physical action of farewell in the rite for the sick pulled me toward Nellie and her history, our history. The decades of caring for Nellie no long felt, as they did at times, to be an epic stretch of futility. We four prayed for Nellie for what she never prayed for herself. The commission of the twenty-third psalm began with anointing Nellie. Words assuring the shepherd's loyal protection took on flesh. The priest dipped his hands in oil and laid them on Nellie's bony forehead and the back of her scraggly hands with the sign of the cross. The gesture soothed the moment and, I hoped, Nellie. The fullness of the sign of the cross was the materiality in the ointment for the soul. The salve rose with the oil's mild smell. Nellie had a nice smell. It was a bit musty.

I appreciated the solemnity and tradition of the formal procedure. Ritual gave shape and depth to my confused feelings. Oil may have been the holy liquid to consecrate ancient priests and kings to the life of service to God, but for me this oil was a balm healing Nellie's wounds. My mother's dying body gave life to plain biblical words promising reconciliation, hers with God and mine with her and Marie and Frank. Physical human action had direct access to the spirit. The imposition of hands called the creator spirit to come and fill the life of the one receiving the sacrament. *Your faith has made you whole.*

For want of a better word, I'll call the effect of the moment hallowing, even though I am not sure what I mean. Maybe *reverential* is a better word, given my caution about the Almighty whose gifts, like his presence—if that's what it was—can be hard to bear. Well, at the very least, I was a witness to something that mattered, and mattered at the end, for the end.

The priest invited us all to hold hands to encircle Nellie and say the Lord's Prayer aloud. Though Frank and I had talked about our difficulties with faith, I'd never discussed religion or prayed with Marie. The condition of Nellie's flesh in the present moment dispelled any awkwardness in me. In fact, I felt part of a communal care. When the prayer asked for our daily bread and forgiveness, the old, worn petitions asked for the very sustenance Nellie's body needed in meeting death.

Nellie's deterioration was not a long good-bye, as some have described the dying of people with Alzheimer's. The valedictory arc of her affliction traced a lengthy advent. As dementia had distanced Nellie from people, so now the healing at death was bringing her closer to us and to the distilled source of life in her. Her persistent losses emerged as the worship to life. Her lifelong self-reliance was yielding to divine-reliance. Not ours, but as Jesus said, "Yours is the kingdom and the power and the glory." Her wizened body seemed to be learning still, preparing for what was next for her, and for us.

Just when I thought all the mothering was coming to an end, Nellie and I were giving rise to more protective care of each other. As had no one before, the final habits of Nellie's consecrated body were teaching me more about my body. When things are taken from us, as life was being taken from Nellie's sinews and lungs, Nellie's body was bidding, "Let them go." These things seemed to have been given to us only to be taken. What is left after everything is gone is, I guess, God, the final nothingness that is everything.

Nellie's physical suffering begged for release. The shallow breathing of Nellie's congested lungs suggested how hard it was for her body to surrender. The hope of the kingdom, if I ever felt that faith, rested on the last effort of Nellie's rasping strains. It sounded like a hunger for air that was her craving for life, new life.

When the priest, a total stranger, offered us the Eucharist, we came more deeply together. We became one in the estrangement of Nellie's dying. Her slightly opened lips that Christine kept moist with Vaseline accepted the crumb of wafer. *Receive, sister, the provision of the body of Jesus Christ and may he preserve you from the malicious enemy and bring you safe to life everlasting.* Marie, Frank, and I took the broken bread with our hands. Like children, we were linked to one another around the foot of our mother's bed. I had no immediate understanding that God was present, but at the age of fifty-two in 1986, I sensed how breaking bread over a dying person could connect people in a mysterious communion. God seems to teach the human heart not by ideas but by pain and contradiction. Hard though it may be to accept the ambivalence of loss and joy, I put my hope in the broken portion of bread, the bread of sorrow, feeding that unseen, yet most wanted, union. The notion of supernatural life in the sacrament seemed peculiar, for we can live it only through the simplest substance of things.

The priest made the sign of peace with a handshake as a goodbye blessing. Then he gently rubbed Nellie's feet before leaving us. Peace in the form of silence settled on Marie, Frank, and me. Nellie struggled for air. Her light pant spoke in our silence for what the sacrament was for her. Her breath condensed life to a gasp.

From the two windows of Nellie's bedroom facing west, the setting sun flooded the entire bedroom. Twilight, Friday late on January 24, 1986, in Cedar Grove, New Jersey, as in scripture, was the beginning of Nellie's new day. Sundown, an exhortation to hope.

Marie, Frank, and I had Swiss cheese sandwiches on Italian bread with milk for supper. There were Entenmann's chocolate chip cookies around that I thought might please as comfort food, but they didn't do the trick. Frank went to sleep at 9:30. Marie went to bed around 10:00. I could not sleep. I washed dishes, then went up the eight steps to Nellie's bedroom and sat in the La-Z-Boy rocker facing her bed. Nellie was unconscious. I kept a weather eye on her. Watching holds the end at bay, briefly.

This was my first death vigil. I watched and almost couldn't bear to watch. But keeping Nellie company was the only comfort I could provide. I tried to be cool and collected. Needless to say, I failed. Foreboding unsettled my effort to relax. What to do when nothing can be done? Aware that hearing was the last sense to go, I thought I might speak to Nellie during her final moments. Words seemed false for a woman who at her most vital was quiet. I was without emotional articulation. I was in the position of a guide who wanted bearings, but there were no rules of the road for this trip. There was only the reality check of Nellie's body to follow. I remained and watched with her. Is that what Paul meant by ceaseless prayer?

For years, Nellie was losing her world. In the bleak early morning hours of Saturday, January 25, 1986, the world was losing Nellie. Nellie's mummified hands rested on her chest. Her breathing strained. Her thin, sallow skin drew tight over her pallid frame. The outline of her veiny skull rose visibly through pellucid covering tissue. Her perfect false teeth were too big for her mouth and head. After months of slow desiccation, Nellie's flesh suddenly turned clammy to the touch. I guess one of death's final throes is heaving up fluids into the wrong places.

When the activity is watching over a dying person, you can be sure that unruly emotions will arise. I tried and failed to manage my imagination. Not to slight my attention to Nellie, but the reaction I had was almost too complex, too big, to accommodate an individual. Scenes changed in sadness as in dreams. A feeling of loss swelled over me in shuddering waves of images. Within Nellie's dying body I pictured the wasting bodies of people lying in St. Vincent's Hospital's AIDS ward and G-9 at Roosevelt Hospital. The fading away of life behind the brows of my mother then spun kaleidoscopically with wan faces of my gay brothers, ancient kinsmen now one with my ancient mother-child. The throng strained Nellie's collective cranium into a massive death's-head.

The story of those suffering from AIDS was no longer complete without a corresponding telling of my mother's pain. In a flash, I was occupying the bony enclosure with the teeming multitude. All were gone or going. Bob, Freddie, Paul, John, Jack, Allen, Donnie, Michael, the others. I would never see them again. The terrible truth is that there is grave beauty when there is nothing left but the spirit of life itself.

Around 3:30 A.M., Nellie's breathing was very shallow. Her respiring sounds to maintain life were like sighs. Now and then, there were deep irregular inhalations. She seemed to hunger for air. Mucus rattled in her throat. Her false teeth clicked. The fluid in her lungs gurgled to the pulses of her slowing arteries. Each gulp of air was shorter than the previous mouthful. Every breath she took was full of my scrutiny. I worried that she would just go on shriveling up with lessening convulsive efforts. But no, her body knew how to die. Nothing was required of me. Her body knew more about dying than doctors, medical textbooks, and my anxious watching could teach me. She put before me the necessary creations and destructions of material nature. Nellie would soon be dust.

In the early sunless morning on Saturday of January 25, 1986, all of Nellie's body slackened in death's chill. Nellie drowned in the fluid that built up her lungs. As her body was the site of vulnerability and trial, so in the end her flesh was the condition of my hope for life's awaiting completion. Will these bones come to life? Silence went straight through me and filled up the room. The occasion was free of any kind of amplified emotion. Will the moment come like this, the time of my death?

* * *

That dim morning when Nellie was lying dead on her bed stays with me as an Edward Hopper painting of estrangement in a known domestic setting. Nellie, Marie, Frank, and I hover in a plain room, staring with custody of the eyes to avert seeing what the others observe, if anything at all is revealed at the time of death. Blankness offers a soft reverence for loss. Human individuality ebbs into a void. The outer and inner worlds merge in the light from the shaded lamp on the bedside table. Its yellow imparts the dazed human figures with a union that transforms the time and place into distilled history. The tableau catches a family narrative at an instant expressing separation with the outcome of the story left to providential foreshadowing.

After Nellie died, I became efficient to stave off grief. I called hospice. The nurse came in the pitch-black of early morning. She made the official death pronouncement and signed the death certificate. She called the undertaker and told him that the family was calm. Funeral directors, I gathered, welcomed knowing what they will encounter when they arrive for the corpse. The nurse expressed her sympathy to Marie, Frank, and me. We thanked her. She left. The funeral director with the help of a local policeman carried Nellie away in a thick dark olive plastic bag that seemed too heavy for its contents. As the twenty-fifth hour burst with activity, so the commotion abruptly ended. The breathless quiet left me slack and empty.

Needing to break the hollow mood, I repaired heavy with sleep upstairs to my adolescent bedroom to lie down and close my eyes. I felt like a nurse who had earned personal rest by having made everything straight. The solace I sought found me. Frank, already in bed, hugged me. In that moment I let fear go. Physical closeness was healing. Through the yielding power of male tenderness our bodies brought back the vigor that death had taken away. Primal pleasure at once revived me and heightened my consciousness. I felt the supreme good will of life, the very ultimate spirit of life, in my unbound lineaments.

Frank and I took rest in each other's arms. Then I went back downstairs to restore Nellie's bedroom to the airy neatness in which she had kept her personal space. For years, Nellie would put sheets and pillowcases out on the backyard clotheslines in the sunshine for an hour or so before making the bed. The brightness in the linens gave a deep satisfaction I could inhale. As a partial nod to Nellie's custom, I stripped the bed and took all the clothes lying around downstairs to the basement for laundering. Nellie's bedroom captured the slow, yellow-powdered morning light. I opened the windows wide. Clean winter air ventilated the sunny room. Lemon Pledge gave the furniture a shine and citron scent. The vacuum swept the carpet. I remade Nellie's bed. A cotton chenille bedspread over tidy yellow sheets freshened everything. It felt good to be useful. Death's dark meant nothing to life's light. Sharp skeins of winter dawn invigorated the air and cleared the gloom.

Wind and sun, good housekeepers, made everything new. Nellie's yellow, her favorite color, was luminous. All was clear once more. The baby-blue sky shone like a sapphire. A gentle force set Nellie free into the young morning. I sat down in the La-Z-Boy. Inner buoyancy caused an ache in my breast that had something to do with a coming to life in the early sunup. I wanted the sun to keep shining, lush and vivid into the afternoon and the evening and the night and the days without end until Nellie roused from sleep in a world totally new and welcoming.

The concrete process of matter captured the destiny of the whole woman in her bodily reality. Nellie was light and air, a radiance out of time that surrendered to the world's absolute horizon. For me, the resurrection of flesh in the eternal present need be nothing more than our return to elemental substances of which the universe is made and goes on making. The end of personal history does not mark the end of existence. The risen body preserves the continuity with our earthly body. That union is deliverance enough for me. It roots death in freedom and expresses a completed coming back home.

The next several days brought matters to a close like the quick curtain of a Verdi opera. The funeral Mass at St. Catherine of Siena Church on Tuesday, January 28, 1986, went by the austere liturgy of the resurrection. No eulogy. No surprises. No verbal embellishments about plain Nellie. Only the lean, unsparing words of scripture filled the air. Nothing got in the way of Nellie's joining the totality of creation. Nellie belonged more to God than to those who loved her.

For our leaving the church after the ceremony, Frank suggested that the organist sing the antiphon *Salve regina, mater misericorde* as a sending forth. *Hail Queen, Mother of Mercy and of Love.* With family, friends, and neighbors following the coffin, the recessional hymn extolled the grace gifts of comfort, care, tender love, and repose.

Any intimation of a perfected life came through accessible and breathing female attributes in the divine nature commended in the *Salve Regina*, those practicalities and nothing more. We walked down the church steps to the hearse to the strong, timeless sound of the medieval hymn honoring a woman like no other. With the casket bearing Nellie's body before us and with Frank on one side of Marie and me on the other side of Marie, the office of motherhood imparted just enough hints to keep me moving in doubt and resistance. It was a matter of bending my will to the needs of others. I could be helpful.

Nellie was not buried with her husband, Salvatore, who died during Eastertide in 1958, and her teenage daughter Florence, who died in July 1937. Their graves were in the Protestant Fairmont Cemetery in Newark. The deaths of her first-born daughter in 1937 and husband in 1958 were behind her. Their graveyard had been left unvisited for uncounted years. For reasons Nellie never explained, she decided one day to drive her green Dodge Duster about twenty miles from her home in Cedar Grove to East Hanover, in Morris County, forty miles from the Giannone burial plot in Newark, to buy a new grave for four bodies in the Gate of Heaven Cemetery, a Catholic cemetery, even though Nellie was not a practicing Catholic.

No one asked Nellie why she bought the new grave with places for four when there was space for herself and Marie in the other cemetery. Marie assumed that the old neighborhood in southwest Newark had so deteriorated after the race riots in the late 1960s that Nellie did not want to return there in death. Marie's explanation made sense, but it struck me as too aesthetic for Nellie's sensibility. Nellie's eye and sentiment were less the center of her character than they were at the service of her private will, which was as unyielding and mysterious as was her disease. Her life was a series of inexplicable and unyielding decisions. Besides, Nellie was a nomad whose wandering feet followed erratic winds. I think of her as continually seeking the place of promised rest.

Certainly when buying the graves she was unaware that the name Gate of Heaven referred to the Mother of God, but the chance Marian associations of maternal nurture and everlasting peace do suit the essential truth of Nellie's life.

Nellie had the soul and destiny of an exile. Though close to her daughter Marie, Nellie lived alone with her pride, casting her lot with her private will. Her goodness arose from her free and lonely decisions. They were the personal eternity in her everyday life. Fittingly, she was put in the separate, alien ground of her late choice. The newly dug dirt in Section 30, Block N, Grave 66 of the Gate of Heaven Cemetery in East Hanover, New Jersey, on the morning of January 28, 1986, was frozen raw underfoot. She knew that she would be buried alone.

She did not know that the church she rejected would give her all that it had to give anyone. Rather than controlling the people of God and pushing seekers around by their fear and longing, the church was there to serve when called upon to offer a consoling hope. In doing so, the religious institution fulfilled the communal trust placed in it by Jesus. Now Nellie joined the mystical wholeness of creation. Of great age, she entered into the great silence of endless morning ahead. In death Nellie became an instrument of the life that for me is God. We all do. We all serve the hidden purpose of creation. That much I hold as truth beneath all my uncertainty about providence.

The morning that Nellie's body was lowered into the icy earth, the space shuttle *Challenger* exploded at 11:39, incinerating seven astronauts in seventy-three seconds. The most substantial things are ready to blow away. The grandest yearnings are on the verge of vaporizing. Everything that is familiar to us is constantly put at risk and taken away. Nothing may be left and we all may evaporate.

The brief graveside liturgy ended when the priest asked that the eternal light shine upon Nellie. The horizon was free of clouds. The hard, gold light of this frosty winter day flashed like leaves in early spring about the gravesite. Nellie's walnut coffin flickered with sun. A praising universe. Each of us surrounding the bier put a droopy red rose on the casket. We walked our separate ways to waiting cars.

8   Of Guilt and Sorrow

I will lead her to a place apart, and will speak to her heart.

—Hosea 2:14

The moment Nellie stopped breathing in the cold, dark early morning of Saturday, January 25, 1986, I got up from the rocker and walked across the hallway to Marie's bedroom to tell her that our mother had died. Curled under a light-blue eiderdown, Marie was sound asleep with her right arm bowed over the pillow against her breasts. Leaning over, I said softly, "Marie, Nellie died." Matter-of-factness and calling our mother by her name, as I had these last years, I hoped, would lighten the news.

Arms shaking, knuckles whitening, Marie loosened her grip of the pillow and silently slid out from under the cover. She came and knelt at the bed alongside Nellie's body. Beneath the quilt Nellie's figure was no larger than a railway tie. She was caught in mid-breath. Her opened mouth sagged her face down, showing perfectly shaped upper and lower false teeth. Her blank eyes were drawn into pellucid flesh marked with bone lines. Marie pressed her face into the mattress. Partly hidden by the bed sheet, my sister's countenance bore resemblance to Greek sculptures of half-veiled women's faces, a sign of mourning. Without moving her head, Marie's palms began fumbling slowly across Nellie's flat chest to find a response, but to no avail. Tears of grief bordering on rage soon flowed uncontrollably. Then Marie shuddered as if a limb were being severed from her body.

Marie's sobbing woke Frank, who was sleeping in the upstairs bedroom. He came to Nellie's bedside and put his right hand on Marie's shoulder. The gesture could not reach her pain. Nellie's years of physical and mental deterioration had not prepared Marie for our mother's slipping into death. Day-in, day-out care of our mother for the past twenty years had taken Marie almost imperceptibly into the desert of dementia. In the end, sharing Nellie's mindscape did to my sister Marie what the desert always does: The bleakness stripped Marie bare of defenses when Nellie died. Marie's face creased, her cracked voice muttering several times to anyone or any deity paying attention: "What do I do now?"

Then she fell into stone silence. The world held only Nellie for Marie.

Marie and I were living two divergent moments on a split-screen at Nellie's deathbed. Marie was partly in the present and partly in the past where decades of caring for Nellie forestalled the dread of our mother's death. I was half in the present and half in the wide-open future where Nellie's life would be completed so that I was set free of care to live my life as I wanted to with Frank.

I was alarmed at Marie's paralysis. I wanted to ask, "What do you mean, 'What do you do now'?" Now you go on living; you are free, home free. You can come and go as you please. You can take winter trips to Florida to see your old friend Clio in Port Saint Lucie. You are sixty-two, you served our mother during your entire life; your life is productive; you have a good position as a teacher and guidance counselor at Union County Regional High School in Springfield, where people value your work; since our father died thirty years ago, you have had the honor of heading a family; you have resources, and you have a measure of health. You have vital years ahead of you. Live! Even though I didn't know what I meant by that. Unable to enter Marie's deep sense of loss, I copped out of responding to her abandonment with a truncated mental version of Henry James's celebrated advice in *The Ambassadors*, "Live all you can; it's a mistake not to."

In silence, I went on saying in phrases filched from potted sympathy to Marie and through her sorrow to mine: Look, you no longer have to worry about how you find Nellie when you wake in the morning. You no longer have to call from school to quiet your doubts about the latest unfamiliar woman hired to be with Nellie during the day. Nellie died in her own bed in her own home with those to whom she gave life. Marie, our mother has found peace. I had misery, hers and mine, all worked out by the cool habits of heart learned as a gay kid to handle the loneliness that threatened to consume me.

These imagined words to Marie were inadequate. I had not grasped the essential fact of my sister's life. Marie had grown up on the Italian-American example of females' taking care of others. Repetitive chores within the same four walls satisfied Marie. She and our mother were contentedly placed together in life, and Marie was happily placed as friend and then provider to our mother. Marie's self-worth was totally invested in another person's welfare. Marie at twenty-eight broke an engagement and never married, to stay with Nellie. When Nellie died, Marie had no sense of herself without that responsibility. Bereavement overtook my sister. Her heartsick body picked up the story that Nellie's left unfinished.

In retrospect as my spirit still comes to terms with the death of my mother over and above the AIDS-related deaths of many friends, I see that Marie had a right to fall apart. Loss of identity is another way of lamenting. Trying to put a cap on my sister's eruption of agonized uncertainty was to shield myself. Would I ever know what my upbeat platitudes hid? Was it love I feared, or did I fear where grief might take me?

Beneath the inrush of conflicting emotions churned unease that if Marie did not have a life of her own she would burden me. A hop, skip, and a jump and she would be wrapped around my neck. I did not want her to weigh me down. A self-protective defense, perhaps, but true to the extent that I was not sure of myself. Marie was the figure of uncontrolled sorrow that only a mother can suffer over her dead child. I did not want to relive the intimacy that rendered me acutely sensitive to my mother's suffering.

I wanted to erect a barrier around the sense of duty that compassion brought. There had to be limits to what and to whom I would give myself. First Nellie, then Marie? There is always another extended hand to hold, another funeral procession needing a shoulder. Does caring keep spooling outward into the world? If so, mothering can be endless, make one a fool. It's one thing to give oneself away, another matter to throw oneself away.

There was Frank to consider. He had willingly pitched in with Nellie's care, but he was also helping his ailing father and aging mother. I could not ask him to take on Marie (which he did without being asked). Concern for Frank was genuine, but protecting Frank was a subtle symptom of my needing to restrict love, a powerful instinct that checked my desire to be useful to Marie. Intimacy was a place where love was dangerous. Once linked to taboo, as it was for a gay kid, human closeness evoked an outsize fear of engulfment. Personal dread and desire, however, contrasted with an appointed plan. I had much to learn about the soul.

In the middle of March 1986, less than two months after Nellie died, Marie was exhausted. It is not unusual for the person who devoted her life to another to delay getting sick until the person being cared for dies. Very much the contained daughter of our émigré parents, Marie, though dog-tired, would not see a physician. Her personal will was a brass barrier between herself and the world. Even her body seemed subject to her volition. In the spring of 1986, however, severe fatigue and jaundice landed her in the emergency room of Clara Maass Hospital in Belleville. Though Marie had no pain, she was hastily diagnosed with obstructive jaundice due to gallstones, a condition usually associated with pain. The attending physician was a know-it-all doctor. Surgery was scheduled to remove Marie's gall bladder. Marie asked what I thought about the plan, and I passively went along with the surgeon's decision.

I met the surgeon, but I didn't look him straight in the eye to see if he was personable or arrogant. That was a mistake on my part. I just wanted the operation over with. Marie trusted me, and I wasn't reliable or vigilant. She submitted to being cut; and I, who had no alternative to reassuring her about the operation, shared in the responsibility. This conceited surgeon removed Marie's gall bladder. Marie recalled hearing during the operation the surgeon discussing his plan to take his speedboat out on Barnegat Bay on the Jersey shore that weekend. It took knives to determine the hepatitis infection that a simple blood test would have shown.

Gall bladder surgery in 1986 went through the body wall and was particularly traumatic for patients with hepatitis. The procedure nearly killed Marie. Without giving details, the surgeon blithely told me after the operation in the hallway that Marie would "probably never leave the hospital." His detached fatalism put the hospital staff into passive resignation about Marie's death. She was left twisting in the wind of mistakes. Callousness added to the enormity of medical blundering. I was at the impasse where Marie had found herself when Nellie died. What do I do now? I wanted to curse their stupidity. But I said nothing because there was too much to say.

The medical staff's acquiescence played to my primitive impulse to respond to immediate threats. The best medical facility in northern New Jersey was at the New Jersey Medical School in Newark. Through the chief of medicine, Francis Chinard, I reached Carroll Leevy, who ran the Liver Institute at the school. By coincidence, Dr. Leevy as a young internist had diagnosed my father's cirrhosis of which he died in April 1958 from the toxic chemicals in the asphalt on which he stood and worked daily for decades. Leevy sent his chief resident, Saad F. Habba, to assess Marie, who was languishing in Clara Maass Hospital.

Dr. Habba, slightly out of shape in an appealing way, greeted me with a prepossessing cherubic face. After he examined Marie and went over her records, Habba's soft face turned sober when he delivered his message to me: Marie had hepatitis B. She had been misdiagnosed and mistreated. Because of the trauma of surgery, Marie had fallen into hepatic-renal syndrome, which is usually a speedy death sentence. This meant another funeral, so soon, too soon, after Nellie's death in January. Frank drove me to Macy's in the Essex Green Mall in West Orange to get a lightweight dark suit that resembled the wool suit I wore for Nellie's winter burial.

Habba won my heart immediately. His simplicity, responsibility, and the touching good manners with which he spoke accounted for his having been chosen chief resident. He clearly explained how the liver was the guardian of the kidneys and that Marie's liver, compromised by surgery, no longer was protecting her kidneys. Her case, for its mismanagement and rareness, was a challenge that the Liver Institute at the medical school would accept. No promises. Fair enough.

Because Marie at this point could no longer participate in her own care, I was making decisions for her. The schedule of treatment was outlined with equal caution and honesty. They would try through temporary dialysis to trick the kidneys into believing that Marie's liver was working. The treatment was slow. Dialysis would buy time for the liver to regenerate, if there were enough healthy cells for the organ to restore itself.

Hospitalization was long and awful for Marie. She was constantly cold, frequently nauseated, bone thin from anorexia, and depressed. Stuck in bed and hemmed in by death, Marie did her best to keep up her dignity while keeping up the morale of those who came to her. Several times she cried to have her hair washed and combed. When I went to her, I looked and I didn't look. Going to the hospital was a form of self-armoring against Marie's anguish. Death and the proximity of death remained the overarching themes of our life. Before the abject exposure of failing life, loyalty alone kept me steady on the jagged line between numbness and dejection.

Newark, a port on the Passaic River, was a modern destination for German, Italian, and Jewish immigrants. During the 1940s and '50s, when I grew up, the city's industries offered blue-collar European families the opportunity to assimilate into American life. With the turmoil of the '60s the city was no longer an entryway into prosperity. By the '80s Newark had become another hostile way station for African-American migrants along their diaspora. The city was old with racism, defeat, decay, and mortality. Through this shattered universe of the civil rights aftermath I went to see Marie in the wreckage of her collapse.

For nearly four months, three or four times a week, I went from our apartment down Hudson Street in the Village to the Christopher Street PATH station for the train to Jersey City and transfer to another train to Newark's Penn Station. There, if rushed, I boarded New Jersey Transit bus 34 to University Hospital to be with Marie. Most of the time I walked up riot-scarred Market Street lined with long-shuttered stores posted with "Closeout Sale" signs and strewn with McDonald's and KFC wrappings. The ruins flickered with vitality. Music rang out from boom boxes. Many pedestrians wore baseball caps fashionably askew. On weekends Frank drove me in. There Marie lay day after day, month after month, in Room 4–11 in the H Green wing. Most of the time Marie was too sick to be comforted. Visitors stopped coming. Get-well cards and flowers went unnoticed. I sat and read, inattentively.

What a difference a knowledgeable chief resident at a teaching hospital made. After several months of competent attention by the medical staff under Habba's watchful eye, Marie survived a dire condition that few outlive. Her recovery was one for the books, and her case may have been written up in a medical journal. I never checked. Marie never saw Habba again. I don't recall her ever thanking him.

But I remember Saad Habba. Let me tell you about him. This physician's direct involvement with the human body taught me about faith. He shared Frank's ability to make me feel better just by being with him. Maybe I had a guy crush on Habba. His medical gifts were enhanced by his humility, an attribute seldom found in academic medicine or the aggressively ambitious Italian-American world, with its show-off sons of packaged masculinity, in which I'd grown up. Habba listened, never pronounced, and always was patiently respectful of the inexplicable human body. He knew when to go forward and when to hold back. If he didn't have ready answers to my questions or if Marie's condition turned worse, this doctor in training had reassurances of his concern.

Habba was an outsider in his profession, and he felt it keenly enough to discuss without restraint his situation as we got to know each other. He was Egyptian in an American medical school of predominantly Jewish, black, and Italian-American colleagues. Although this New Jersey medical school did not rank among prestigious national institutions, it partook of the snobbery that in advance equates academic pedigree with individual competence. Hopkins, Columbia, and suchlike were not part of Habba's education and training. He'd studied medicine in Ireland, regarded, I gathered, as a cut above the

Caribbean and Mexican alternatives for Italian Americans from New Jersey who were denied admission to American medical schools.

Habba was the other, the foreign interloper who was looked down upon simply because he'd arrived at the school by an unfamiliar foreign route that didn't pre-stamp him as smart. But he was well trained and well chosen to be chief resident by the head of the Liver Institute and knew his medicine without displaying expertise in that competitive way in which physicians pull rank. Marginality served Habba well. He, a Middle Eastern healer with a vestigial Irish accent, did not practice from the hierarchal center of the medical school pecking order; and his patients were all the better for his personal estrangement, theirs by illness, his by ethnicity. Success for Habba was in his patients' welfare rather than in personal prestige. Because he believed a patient's well-being depended on her or his family as well as on medical science, Habba kept an eye out for how information could involve relatives. He took care of Frank and me.

Sensitivity carried over to Habba's dealings with older colleagues. With the senior physicians at Clara Maass Hospital who'd bungled Marie's diagnosis, Habba offered no overt or snide criticism for their not running the hepatitis test that had obviously been indicated. He simply arranged for Marie's transfer to the medical school. Medicine, whether one is patient, visitor, or practitioner, is a way to experience class in America. At the Liver Institute the nursing staff responded with the thoughtful respect that Habba showed for their hands-on work. On a number of occasions I was there for medical rounds, which Habba conducted with warm praise for the students who had the correct answer and a calm understanding for those who didn't or who remained silent. While mentoring younger medical students, Habba taught me how interior habits of modesty bear fruit in the art of healing. As the other, Habba identified with the otherness of patients, who are always the outlanders in a medical setting. Service patients, the poor, who made up the majority in Newark, and insured patients received equal attention. Habba did not practice medicine refracted through a prism of fee and class. Nor did he seek adulation. He was the cultural anomaly who set the professional norm.

Because so few survive hepatic-renal syndrome, Habba took with Marie more than his usual personal interest in patients. He treated her like a complete human being even when she was nearly comatose and sullen—symptomatic of severe liver disease rather than her obstinate nature—to Habba. Marie's lack of expressed appreciation didn't lessen his sympathy for her condition. Busy as he was supervising residents and fellows, Habba took time to explain to me the daily reports of blood tests so that I could participate in Marie's care by understanding the slow stages of her disease and improvement, if that would develop. He taught me how particular enzymes indicated liver function and how creatinine clearance would show if Marie's kidneys were responding to the ploy of dialysis. Unlike his senior colleagues who practiced laboratory medicine of charts away from patients and dealt in condescending statements and verdicts, Habba frequently remarked how little he knew about the workings of the human body.

I don't want to put a halo on Saad Habba. Then again, maybe I do. Within the limited context of professional consultations, he and I exchanged quite a few details of our personal lives—he about his foreign training, I about living with Frank in the Village. When Frank was with us, Habba acknowledged him as my partner. I sensed beneath Habba's formality and gentle humor an inner life rooted in a reverence for the mystery of flesh and life itself.

Habba became for me the human being with feelings and aspirations that individual patients were to him. As they were not mere cases, he was not the Doctor, titled, aloof, and magisterial. Habba knew isolation—his, the patient's, and the family's—and he sought to ease it. It never occurred to me in 1986 to consider if he was Muslim; but now that Islam and Islamic virtues are so much in our awareness, I wonder if the unassuming belief in himself came from his belief in the peaceful, compassionate Koranic God. Conceivably, Habba could have been a Christian Copt. He did embody the gentle fervor associated with the Copts' ancient form of Orthodox religion.

In that respect, this Egyptian doctor reminded me of another Middle Eastern attendant of the sick from an adjacent desert place, Dorotheos of Gaza, who ran an infirmary in the desert in the early sixth century. For both men, it was a daunting mission of stark, terminal physical trials in a bleak place with death in the balance. Dorotheos means "gift of God," an epithet that doubles for Habba's timely intercession in Marie's life. The great virtue of the sixth-century solitary who nursed the sick in the desert was humility. Habba did not have to put into words his beliefs to impress me with his trust in the hidden sources of life. Religion aside, like the ancient desert helper of the sick, Habba had that special strength of not giving way to discouragement from the sickness before him, his profession, and his patients. Habba's enemy was death; his ally, life itself.

Saad Habba won the battle over Marie's disease, but he did not conquer Marie's intransigence. She was his star patient, one who recovered from a usually fatal disease. And she rebuffed him. After she left University Hospital, she would not see him for necessary follow-up consultations. Habba knew more about her condition than any physician ever would. That knowledge terrified Marie. She would rather have been forced into being treated by unfamiliar emergency room doctors who would never again see her than have her body and willfulness viewed in the exposing light of vulnerability and gratitude.

After finishing his fellowship at the medical school, Habba opened a private practice in gastroenterology at Overlook Hospital in Summit, New Jersey, within driving distance from Marie's home in Cedar Grove. He sent Marie his card. That was in 1986. Until Marie died in 2003, the card remained untouched with assorted get-well greetings and junk mail in the fluted silver tray by the phone near the front door of Marie's living room.

When Marie returned home from University Hospital, she went to Nellie's bedroom. Marie changed bedrooms because hers, over the garage of the split-level house, was drafty in winter. Nellie's room was over the furnace and warmer. The move made sense. Even so, I worried if Marie was going to become Nellie by merging into care-receiver to preserve her relationship with our mother. Marie's recovery would be slow and long. I carried within me an unclouded picture of solemn duty to my sister. I would visit her home to fulfill my obligation as brother. I naïvely assumed that recuperation would bring Marie back to her vital self, but I soon saw that a lengthy hospitalization had taken its toll on her mind.

At first the impairments were slight: forgetting to pay bills, not opening mail, and needing help with her income taxes. Never much of an acquirer, Marie became a bit of a hoarder of small things, not just photographs with sentimental meaning but useless scraps such as old newspapers and shabby clothes. When I organized or threw away items, she became angry. Then I realized that I tidied the place for me, not her. The stress of cognitive decline took form in Marie's attaching value to all kinds of objects in which she displaced anxiety and fear. While accepting the atmosphere of clutter, I became anxious about what this orderliness forebode. After all, I was going to be the one to deal with it when something, anything, happened.

Going to Marie, my sad feet bore old fears. During the week, when I got off the 8:45 P.M. New Jersey Transit bus 195 from New York on Pompton Avenue in Cedar Grove, would I find Marie fallen on the floor, as I'd sometimes found Nellie? If Marie became Nellie, would I become Marie?

Looking into the future, I saw dying nerve cells littered with strange deposits shriveling up Marie's brain. To my partial medical understanding, dementia seemed to follow the course of privation as the system that carries nutrients, once damaged, effectively starves the brain cells to death. This was the journey of blocked neural pathways taken by our grandmother and mother. Marie was showing early signs of memory impairment and change in behavior and personality. Given our genetic history and the stress of Marie's caring for Nellie, my sister was at risk for Alzheimer's disease. I did not want to be back in dementia world, from which death is the only exit.

Discharge from the hospital did not change Marie's nature or disposition. Frail and fretful, she was as combative as ever. With every ounce of residual might, she took the path of most resistance. The first person to feel the brunt of her opposition was the visiting nurse who came to see how Marie was doing at home. Marie told the woman not to bother returning because she was managing just fine. Dismissing the nurse showed Marie to be most humorous when she was least aware. She refused outside help for cleaning and cooking, everyday jobs that she couldn't physically handle. Being saved from death brought neither gratitude nor revaluation. She wanted to live by her will so much that she took up residence in her head, where she could not die or even be sick or dependent. Illness made her more intensely herself.

The predicament surrounding Marie's recovery comprised everything that reset the framework of my life: people, things, and events large and small. Their totality did not take shape from my will. Like Marie, I had to face the hard facts of life. The circumstances held enigma and contradiction. The people life put at my side, the places, the time, health and sickness, the scourge of HIV, the interplay of events—all of these forces that molded me, burdened me, or buoyed me—made me concurrently rebellious and obedient.

As when Nellie was sick, the round of New Jersey household chores during the late 1980s and early 1990s continued to give me a sense of usefulness at a time when I felt helpless against the persistent devastation of HIV surrounding me in the city. Chelsea and the Village were a canvas for slow death and disfigurement. Sadness lurked in agreeable pastimes. A casual walk could abruptly hit a heart-smashing wall. That happened one spring Saturday afternoon. I went up to browse through the West 17th Street Housing Works thriftshop. While thumbing through racks of men's clothing, I found myself sliding many hangers of suits and coats all in the same size and snazzy style with upscale labels. And then my blood ran cold at these sure signs of a recent wholesale donation from an estate of a fashionable man at the top of his professional career.

Dying young people remained the new normal in pestilential ZIP codes 10003, 10011, and 10014. Haggard, boyish figures with canes labored up and down Hudson Street and Eighth Avenue. Some hobbled off the elevator into our third-floor hallway as daily reminders of my personal history and responsibility. Allen across our hall in Apartment 3S, Paul in 3R down the hall, and John in 3P farther down the floor kept deadly disease at my door. One by one, each neighbor thinned into disappearance. The ghost of each spooked me. Preferring anxiety to knowledge, I was too fearful to get tested. I was more like Marie in denial than I would admit. But I owed Frank the truth of my status, which in August 1989 was negative. It was hard to take *yes* for an answer.

Even if released from the immediate threat of HIV, I felt trapped in the habits and yearning of a lifetime. Far from being a final victory, coming out as gay at Fordham, like falling in love, was only the beginning of the emotional work of loving another person and finding my true self. No doubt about it, being openly gay at a Catholic Jesuit university brought considerable professional freedom with students and colleagues. But this liberty was not enough. One more challenge, a primal discontent, nagged me. Self-realization involved something more, more than myself, more than my relations, more even than the known world. I longed for the freedom of faith that for me brought the freedom to love.

From the onset of Marie's hepatic-renal syndrome in 1986 to her death in 2003, I followed the worn road to planet Giannone that I had taken since 1967, the year I moved from northern Indiana to New York. The Cedar Grove house was the same. Yellow towels in the green-tiled bathroom, yellow sheets on the bed next to the light oak night table, Farberware in the kitchen, rarely used Waterford crystal in the china cabinet. Small things had histories. Going home was checking painful memory against present reality and getting a jolt: They squared.

Marie took to isolation as a bear seeks hibernation. A once-friendly woman who was part of the town's post–World War II new development and greeted people from the driveway was becoming the Garbo of the neighborhood. Being alone suited her lower social energy and increased her talent for getting others to do things for her without having to feel indebted. Her independence depended on the generosity of several neighbors, none of whom got close to her. She assigned me the job of doorkeeper. Bound by her orders, I would go just so far in abetting her self-management. My trans-Hudson relationship to Marie was a holding action against her physical collapse.

I can't pin down what sickness meant to Marie. By her lights, she was not supposed to be sick. When she was, she felt that her body had betrayed her. As remedy, her iron will took over to teach her body how to be healthy. Empowered by this determination, Marie would bring her friable liver and mushy lungs up into her head where her notion of health preserved her from fear. If her stoicism was genuine, the strengths forged in illusion made life difficult. I admired her control while despairing of it. The thrust of her will amounted to a flight from her body. The sicker she became, the more she insisted that she was not her body. She was someone stronger, imprisoned in flesh and heroic in daily action. Because her body had deceived her, Marie became suspicious of life itself. Illness gave Marie a great deal of psychological power, and she used it. She spoke a silence that can be described only as Marie, part accusing, part imploring, totally disconcerting.

Marie avoided physical contact. She accepted an embrace or a kiss from Frank and me when we arrived because these gestures lingered from the familial past. When lesions on her left calf seeped fluid, she let me wash the sores until the ooze stopped. The warm, soapy water in the blue plastic bucket taken home from a hospital stay that soaked her feet made her feel and look better. Marie's skin was dying from lack of touch. Now and again she would allow me to comb her hair, after which she would immediately brush it to get rid of my touch. Marie needed to sweep away the shame of receiving from others the help she needed. The wave of her hand initially seemed a reproach, but like many of her reactions the motion in time signaled to my own spiritual pride that Marie was checking. I was embarrassed about accepting inner guidance and seeing God as helper. But who else protects us against the demons of egocentricity in the desert of grave sickness? Positive self-regard follows on the heels of modesty and submission. I would like to live and love from within simplicity of heart.

One Saturday afternoon in June 2002, our cousin Kathy was giving a party twenty miles away in Edison to celebrate her son's high school graduation. These are big outdoor family affairs. In preparation, I called the nearby beauty parlor on Pompton Avenue, La Diva Italiana, to see if they could take Marie for a much-needed shampoo and haircut. The woman answering the phone was relaxed about the last-minute call on a busy Saturday and told us to come right over. Frank and I cajoled Marie into going. We'd no sooner arrived at the hairdresser's than Marie wanted to leave. Getting gussied up was too much for my sister. A slight figure, now down to about 110 pounds, Marie wanted to vanish completely.

The salon had the felt camaraderie of suburban Italian-American female regulars who obviously enjoyed long Saturday visits with one another away from males. The day for them was as much social as it was cosmetic. Everything was arranged for collective pleasure. The salon chairs were more chaise longues. Coffee and miniature Italian pastries were on a corner table. By gender and ethnic kinship, the patrons in this little Saturday world of flourishing women in their sixties, seventies, and beyond spotted Marie as one of them, and as a more defenseless *sorella*, sister, in a stronghold for the frail. They greeted Marie with genuinely polite smiles and hellos.

The voices of these women were worn, to be sure, like their faces and hair. No physical sweetness was left in the way they spoke to one another. But there was another kind of timbre in their words; a kindness, lenience, a patient understanding. They gave freshness to conventional remarks and ethnic clichés. These women somehow knew that things would fall apart if coarsely handled. A heavyset woman of sixty-something in a navy blue sweatsuit, variously called Angie then Angela or just Ange, oversaw the resetting of her blond wig. She was bald, from chemotherapy, I guessed, and confined to a wheelchair; and yet her raspy voice fully and humorously enlivened the banter. At one point, a twenty-something woman with long frizzed hair sprinted out of a crimson Toyota SUV and dashed into the flutter of it all. She'd come to get her silvery-blue-coiffed grandmother. Everyone knew that they were headed to a 4:00 P.M. wedding at St. Catherine of Siena Church down the street. Though also on the way to a party, Marie remained withdrawn from all this social anticipation. The women understood. It went without saying that pressure had no place in this day spa. They knew better. I didn't. I pushed Marie into getting a haircut and going to the party. Mother, me, thought he knew what was good for her.

How did I know what would bring Marie pleasure? What was it like for her to be taken against her wish from one lost world to another? Marie may have felt a sense of loss wherever she went that Saturday afternoon in June. Perhaps Marie didn't feel a sense of loss.

As Marie's body weakened, her spirit strengthened. Her will fortified her against past and future pain and any immediate reminder of her frailty. One morning when Marie was shaky on her feet tottering to the bathroom, I went so far as to lift her physically to help her bathe, as I'd routinely picked up Nellie. Marie said with toneless resentment, "Get away." Whenever she felt pushed around, Marie turned into dry ice. Then, if I touched her, I was never sure if I'd been burned or frozen.

Just below the surface, Marie and I were living on our nerves. Frank's kindness was the bridge between us. Marie understandably preferred his presence to mine. Her true friend, however, was solitude; her frequent companion was loneliness. Sitting in the upholstered chair by the living room window looking over the newspaper, Marie gave the impression of intuitive faith in herself, something of implied confidence of constancy, safety, and acquitted from the harmful effects of disease.

From Marie's near-fatal illness in 1986 to her death in 2003, we soldiered on. Years after her death I still am at war with myself, always will be. It is not one struggle but many. It is not one will but several vying at once. The essential conflict takes place in the combat zone of my heart. I want to serve and help while wanting things my way. The enemy is my personal will wanting to impose itself on the desires and needs of others, and on God's ways. This was the dark side of mothering, its overbearing surveillance, which I developed. Even moral duty fell under my resolve. Along with the prescriptions in the medicine cabinet, I believed that caring for the sick came with an expiration date.

I tried to see the situation from Marie's viewpoint, but I couldn't sustain the perspective. Putting Marie's sense of what she needed, even when unreasonable and detrimental, above my wishes required a humility I lacked. But another modesty was taking hold. In my late sixties (imagine!), I had a glimpse of myself as being like everyone who performs ordinary tasks that had to be done for others. For a gay man who had always felt outside conventional family life, humility—seeing myself as no different from any one else—was a new way to achieve self-worth.

The final months of my nursing Marie took root in the need to cultivate such hard surrender. To enter into this kind of kinship was not a faint-hearted venture. Such an intimacy meant fighting my need for solutions to her problems. Perfectionism was a trap. I knew beforehand by her emotional signals that to suggest medication for depression was such an insult to her self-control as to be unthinkable. I was too trusting in the pharmaceutical companies' commercials to take in her wisdom in resisting the next-best drug that didn't work. Actually, so little worked when caring for Marie that accepting failure became a success. I settled for being useful, sometimes useless. Life and God would do the rest.

Marie submitted to solitude, illness, and unavoidable necessity without complaint. Pampering annoyed her. Coddling, she felt, was for men, all of whom were babies to her. She expressed anger but never whined. Rather, she covered emotional slumps with forced enthusiasm. When loneliness and heavy fatigue from shortness of breath set in, and loss of easy movement dejected her, as they would anyone, Marie drew silence over herself just as she burrowed under her eiderdown quilt for comfort. Her darkest moments were simply and bearably her quietest moments.

Her resistance was sending a message about managing existential anxiety and fear, both hers and mine. So what if she didn't take her medication? All those poetic names of dancing double compounds to boost up her heart—Digoxin, Digitoxin, and Deslanoside—capped off with Aricept as a pirouette for her sluggish brain actually made her feel less in control, more afraid. Did it matter that she was belligerent? I did not have to like her; I had to help her. But how? From the hidden ground of love to which Marie was receding, her illness issued a silent call to be loved so that she could continue to love, and I could learn to love anew.

Marie could amaze. Before the evidence of perishing life, she thought of herself as being safe and sound, managing by her own devices in her own home. Home was safety and freedom. The house turned inward, like a fort or cloister bolted against the outside world. In this preserve, she overcame all forms of doubt and disease by exercise of will. Snow filled the driveway; she let it stay. (Joe next-door and his sons plowed it.) The refrigerator broke down and leaked; she didn't ask for help. Food and drink? Don't ask. She fractured her left arm; she accepted the pain rather than go to the emergency room. She could heal the splintered bone by repairing her self-image. Her indifference to pain at times befitted the ascetic Greek stoic Zeno. I was feeling less and less Marie's seclusion from the world than I felt my separation from her.

But again, did my unawareness of the shifts rocking her inner life matter at this point? Information may have eased my ignorance, but it did nothing for Marie. Her body knew more about aging and illness than any psychological insight or medical opinion could provide. Besides, doctors in the recent past had nearly killed her in misdiagnosing hepatitis for gallstones, and this had sent Marie on the downward spiral to the infirmity she was living out.

Marie undoubtedly remembered how useless the horrible spinal tap on our aged mother had been in halting the plagues entangling Nellie's brain. Nellie's trials with no payoff followed by Marie's botched diagnosis and treatment left me with a healthy skepticism about medical wisdom. Her nagging coughs were here to stay. Now it seemed wise to deal more with what congestive heart failure meant to Marie than with the physical effects of pulmonary insufficiency. This was not a case of illness as metaphor but of illness as one of many truths of Marie's life. If I were to continue helping Marie, I would have to go softly on the foundation of love that undergirded her life with Nellie. Marie's love was the truest kind, unseen but felt in Nellie's peaceful death.

Together, Marie, Frank, and I developed an etiquette that honored Marie's denial that she needed help. Two or three days during the week, I took the 195 bus Cedar Grove that rolled along New Jersey Route 3, the fairly unremarkable highway that opened the floodgates of my unsettling history, physical and moral. On Friday evenings, Frank and I drove in. On our way over, I called Marie to ask if Frank and I could visit. Yes, that was fine. We arrived as guests bearing food and small gifts of enthusiasm. With the finer delicacy of host, Marie allowed for our visits. This reciprocal propriety during her final months gave access to a deeper intimacy growing among us.

To this day I cannot tell what we were working out. Nevertheless I could admire and rejoice even when I was in the dark. The little I knew for sure was that Marie in her late seventies was at her best alone. In solitude she had no need to spruce up. Nor did she have to expend emotional energy to be sociable. In her world of one, she never failed others or herself. The body she sought to forsake served as the barricade against being figured out. Because she had decided to allow no room for anything that shamed or frightened her, she became shrouded in mystery. Important issues were left for another day. That indefinite day of crisis came, and it came twice during her final months.

In the early afternoon on the first of May in 2003, Marie fell from her bed and injured her upper right arm. I was at work. Our elderly Aunt Em, staying with Marie, tried to help lift Marie up and could not. Nor could Marie get herself up. Over Marie's protests, an ambulance took her to St. Barnabas Medical Center in Livingston. The fracture was not a full break, but fluid from chronic pulmonary insufficiency and the threat of congestive heart failure warranted hospitalization for several days. Unable to live by herself, and unwilling to have a live-in woman share her house, Marie, on May 7, 2003, was admitted to St. Vincent's Nursing Home near her Cedar Grove home for three weeks of rehabilitation.

Marie's fierce will boomeranged. The social worker at St. Barnabas Hospital told the nursing home that Marie was so uncooperative in her insistence to live alone at home that the staff used a posey, a mild restraint or soft straitjacket, to keep her in bed. (They also gave her a psychotropic drug not to help her but to calm her feistiness and ease their work.) The nursing home accordingly assigned Marie to a bed in the locked unit (yes, the cuckoo's nest) on the ground floor. To open the door, one pressed code "1939"—memorable as the year Germany invaded Poland. Entering this area unnerved me. A mute resident whose spine was permanently bent over at the waist to a ninety-degree angle roamed from room to room dusting everything in sight. Another resident, a former urologist, grinned as he constantly rubbed his crotch. There were erratic, soul-rasping outbursts from rooms; and there were pockets of dead silence.

Although the setting was badly chosen for Marie, I did not want to start out on the wrong foot with the staff. Marie needed them. Each time I punched 1939 to open the door to the locked ward, I held my breath. Just what trials was Marie enduring? Fortunately, the nurse practitioner at St. Vincent's soon realized that Marie was not disruptive or mentally unbalanced and placed her with recovering residents on the second floor. With competent care, Marie developed an appetite. But she was battling more than chronic bronchitis, congestive heart failure, and depression from sedentary confinement. The stronger she got, the more insistent she became about returning home. Getting home was all she talked about. *Home*, I was learning, was a word highly charged for Marie with a security it never had for me.

To a seventy-eight-year-old woman who enjoyed the smell of grass and took for granted the right to move about her house and back yard now blossomed with pink and white roses, spending this May in an airless room was being, she said, "in jail."

Nursing homes are like jails. Full of disease, rigid procedures, and disheartening. Not a day went by that she did not call me from the nurse's station to get her out. She did her best to disconnect from captivity. Revved by barely controlled anger, Marie was cold to the staff and formally courteous with the other residents, as if she were a visitor passing through. She was furious. The atmosphere was impersonal. The work of the staff, if humanly worthy, was so basic and repetitious and the patients' outcome of their effort so predictably negative that the staff changed frequently. At best one hoped for a businesslike demeanor from the personnel.

Frank and I went regularly to St.Vincent's. Each visit followed a pattern of eagerness to see one another that was dashed by disappointment. A few minutes in, I was hit with an appeal I couldn't satisfy. Marie greeted me with, "Oh good, you're here to take me home." I defaulted to bedside palaver about her returning home "when you are ready."

At these words Marie's eyebrows went up, and her eyes flashed craftily. One did not outfox Marie. The ruse was beneath us both. She must have sensed my wish that her arrangement at St. Vincent's would be permanent. Silence pushed her back in the chair. She gave me a swift look and then turned her anger directly on me. I was one of the jailers torturing her with false hopes of release. Marie's big, dark voice issued marching orders: "Go home!"

A wall of sound shut down the visit. The consequences of Marie's scorn were latent in every step I took out the door. As I left, I felt in her blunt dismissal depths below it I hadn't plumbed. Illness allowed Marie to push the dimensions of her private will down to the subdued dignity securing her wrath. Big sister was a commandant in baby-blue slippers.

Her cracked heart cut mine. In raw, radical form her struggle for freedom from impoundment expressed mine. I wanted to be free of being captive to her illness. I wanted Marie to stay at St. Vincent's where the care was good. But how did I know what was best for her? Or for me? Without putting myself in my sister's place, my attempts to understand were destined to fail. Marie's anguish was so intense that any protestations from me, even of love, were out of place. Simply to stand by her would be enough, I thought. I was wrong, again.

"Get me out of here," she demanded one Saturday in May as the three of us walked down the second-floor corridor for privacy to chairs in a windowed corner. Here we go again. Well, not exactly. The probability of remaining at St. Vincent's was no match for beat-the-odds Marie. Vehemence molded her facial muscles. "They think they own my body." Her fury was precise. Her intensity was fearless. "How would you like it if people watched you every minute of the day?"

Recovery meant more than being able to walk and breathe; strength for Marie demanded reclaiming her body as her own. She pointed to a room with a person taking nutrition by tubes. "Look, this place, this nursing home, has rules that they force on people all the way to death." Apparently she'd also heard about or glimpsed a failed attempt to resuscitate a resident. "They broke an old woman's ribs the other night to save her heart, and she died anyway." Then, Marie let go in full cry, "Get me out!" A detainee at Guantánamo could not have been more vehement. God had given her passion. I was thankful for that.

I had heard the mandate many times before, but it seemed new. Marie's voice grabbed me like a hook in my heart. Her grievance insisted that I feel her pain of incarceration. The entire world seemed waiting for my reply. Never has my loyalty been so tested and my heart so probed as by her call for freedom. As a gay man whose body was defined by social control, I took in her protest. Her defiance went to the core of how I felt about my own body and who owned it. I was sick and heartbroken all at once. I felt sadness and fear of tomorrow.

When Frank and I returned early evening that Saturday to our apartment in the Village, I was still shaken. By 2003 Frank had been with me for twenty-two years. Our partnership was repeatedly tested in the fire of social defiance and in the emergency room with family members and each other. Characteristically, Frank spoke not a word. He put down the bags with clean laundry, pulled me against him, and held me tight. Frank's grip was so firm that his Parkinson's got his arms wedged hugging me. We were caught, locked, immovable. We laughed. The sinews of our attached muscles held the love that bound us through the tight spot with Marie.

I was home. I was in my faithful friend and partner's shelter.

Marie's longing for release from miserable isolation slowly cut through my emotional jumble. Yearning for home was one thing; dying from yearning was unthinkable. In my deep heart, I believed that if Marie surrendered to institutionalizing of her life, the cloud of depression would color all her thoughts and emotions gray. A vibrant woman would slip into the hopelessness and subservience she'd fought all her life. Trapped in the nursing home, Marie was assailed by adversaries in various forms. The timid and angst-ridden residents shuffling in walkers through the hallways haunted her as ominous inhuman fates.

At St.Vincent's she was lonely against her will. This isolation meant defeat. Being home alone, however, was neither new nor displeasing for Marie. At home on Harper Terrace, she would be solely dependent on the source of her life; she would be alone with the Alone. Chosen aloneness held out the possibility of transforming her sickness and dying into the chance for new inner growth, perhaps a new occasion of love. It would be a wracking struggle, but Marie was made for combat. Perhaps there was only one kind of freedom, and it came about when she could be on her own within the fifty-year-old walls of her own split-level Cedar Grove home that she'd inherited from Nellie. Contrary to Marie the prisoner locked up getting medical attention against her will, Marie the liberated solitary in her cell of choice would have to confront her fate with her own inner resources. This was interior warfare to the end. St. Vincent's was not as safe as it seemed, nor was home. Storms trouble every safe harbor.

Whatever course I decided to follow was as much a muddling through my uneasy ambivalence as it was for managing my sister's condition. With a relative's help I found Debbie, a woman who was experienced with sick and dying people. Once again our socially insular family relied on a black person. Debbie would need tried-and-true strength, for she would have much to bear living with Marie. Debbie came early Monday morning and left Friday evening when Frank and I arrived. We stayed until Sunday late afternoon. Marie had Sunday evening and night to herself. It was a rocky pact. Marie frequently told "the woman," as Marie called her, in no uncertain words, to leave. Happily, Debbie took Marie's hostility as part of the job. At St. Vincent's, Marie was interested only in getting home; when she got home, she was interested only in being alone. Solitude made her feel whole.

My attending Marie confined to the family home during her final months was for me a further departure from the modern world. The venture took me back through the desolate high wilderness of the Abruzzo Mountains where our family originated and still further back to the desert of late antiquity, the sparse world in which the desert mothers sought a way to God.

* * *

June 23, the day Marie left St. Vincent's, through September 4, 2003, were Marie's final days. The course for her was inevitably a discovery of loss, which is so much a part of meeting the divine. Having a stranger in the house meant the loss of privacy. Shared space meant loss of control. Being shut in caused sensory deprivation. Not having a watchful nursing staff around took its toll. Marie's breathing shortened; her walking lessened as her steps contracted; and her appetite bated.

Every loss, so alarming one day, became inescapable fact the next. Compensations filled in the deficits. Marie stayed alert. She clung to who she was; she fought to be who she is. In the heat of battle, loss set something free in her—and in me. Weak, halting, frightened were not Marie. Underneath her pale skin laid victory in the stalk of her neck and the fixed way she held her drooping shoulders. Rather than drift away, Marie went out to meet suffering. She wanted to go where no one else wanted to be. She remained an integral part of life and my life as a child under my care.

Marie's inner life did thrive during the late stages of debility. As disease lingered, she led a bold life. Her soul learned from her body. She accepted the physical facts of illness that she had vehemently denied. Actually, what I interpreted as denial was Marie's refusal to be her disease. A simple but hard-won realism relaxed and redirected her struggle. The fight was not against her body but for life. Her weakened heart and lungs seemed not betrayals but subtle proofs of a deeper and enduring life. In some eccentric way, her subdued body brought humility to her spirit, her essential self. Her élan, nothing artificial, kept her feisty, confident, and annoying. "I'm fine," was her response to anyone who asked how she was doing. She spoke the truth.

It was late Sunday in mid-August, when Marie seemed freer than she had been. Frank and I were preparing to return to New York. Marie, wearing a pea-green sweatshirt to keep warm even in August, was sitting on the top of the eight steps that led from her bedroom down to the living room. As I was heading out the front door carrying things to the car, I heard her risk with Frank a feeling that she'd withheld from me. Arms folded with her legs clasped in her arms and chin on her knees to brace herself, she said to Frank, "I could not have done it without you boys."

Her words hallowed the meal and the day. Marie was another woman. New to me but probably recognizable to Nellie and a merciful God. It was okay that I wasn't supposed to know how much Frank and my partnership meant to her. Marie's guarded recognition aroused a fundamental, ineradicable feeling of kinship among the three of us.

The old fire in Marie's belly kindled her heart, and us boys. A chastened ease settled on our imminent departure. Seemingly the neediest of people and also the most emotionally opaque, Marie was capable of being extravagantly transparent. Beneath her quirks shone the underlying kindness that had nurtured her care for our mother. Frank noticed that Marie's eyes, usually searching, were quiet. She risked the danger of exposing her deep self that united us. Gratefulness took the chill from her shivering bones. From the corner of my eye I saw that she wasn't smiling. I trusted the personal warmth. As happened with my mother, while Marie's cognitive functions diminished, her spiritual brain kept, even gained, supple power. She was fully present to what was going on. Transparency added a quiet weight to her words of thanks. Her concern for us boys released a power that remains. From the midst of trial, her appreciation came to me as a blessing. The joy pained me. I felt affection for the sense of loss that her frailty presaged.

Marie's soul was advancing. My sister was becoming a new woman. Marie was gentle with herself. Marie's appreciation that Sunday gestured toward a bold trust in casting herself for aid before life and the creator of life. The moment reduced everything to essentials. Instead of talking about what mattered, we three were aware of it.

Marie turned seventy-nine on Saturday, August 30, 2003. Though sadness accompanies a birthday celebration for a sick elderly person, there were reasons to make merry. Marie's being home called for celebration. The sun was shimmering hot, the way Marie, always cold in the bone, liked her days. I put out chairs and folding tables under the maple tree in the back yard for a birthday gathering. Marie wore a white blouse with blue slacks. Rose Gallo, a family friend going back all seventy-nine years to the tightly knit Italian-American Newark enclave, came for dinner, typically set for 4:00 in the afternoon. Rose wore a lilac pantsuit and wide-brimmed straw hat. She brought Russell Stover dark chocolates. The menu was my Saturday fare of chicken thighs and red potatoes roasted to a crisp, which never let me down.

Marie was energetic. When Rose needed a sturdy pillow to support her back in the wired chair I set, Marie with a spring in her step went inside the house to get a throw cushion. The conversation between Marie and Rose was light, effortlessly respectful. They knew when to smile, which was frequently. The old ethnic neighborhood brought out the best in them. As usual, their blended voices were busy with the past. They ate it up. So did I. The talk between two Italian women of a certain age, *due vecchie*, expressed not wistful exaggeration but knowing humor about how things were for daughters of immigrants, and weren't. The way they listened to each other struck me as another way of loving and healing between aged Italian-American females. From women in suburban attire came reaffirmations of the old country that neither woman ever saw and still made their own.

From time to time, Marie got up to make sure that Rose had a fresh paper napkin or to refill her wine glass to brave effect. Serving was her way of showing spine. She held herself deliberately, aware of our attention and responding to it. As times past were in her voice, personal history was in her gait. A bit stooped, somewhat slow, but standing tall, Marie did not carry herself like a victim; she walked with a purpose.

Around 5:00 that afternoon, after helping his ailing mother in Belleville, Frank joined us. He had a way of approaching familiar company that cast a spell of generosity. His boyish beam and kiss cheered Marie and Rose. He brought fresh *cannoli* and those flaky clam-shaped *sfogliatelle* filled with ricotta from Ferrara's, the last authentic Italian *pasticceria* on Bloomfield Avenue in Newark. Frank was another brother-mother to Marie, one brother happily not rankled by family history. Amity overtook the fine taste of the pastries. Rose left two hours later so that she could drive the four miles in summer daylight to her apartment in Little Falls. Marie washed dishes. Frank and I tidied the house up before leaving for Manhattan.

This was the hardest hour—the evening of departure. Marie would be alone with her private sorrows until Debbie came Monday morning, when Marie would be more alone with the unwelcome companion. With or without people, Marie would be sorely tested by her failing body. But it was her gaunt body that was a home within her home for the coming of faith. I loved her rebellious pride in her physical self-governance, with all its occasions of absurdity. That birthday, Marie scored a victory against loneliness and the nursing home.

As we were leaving via the front door, Marie thanked Frank and me for coming. We thanked Marie. She sat on the top step of the front brick stoop of the house to extend the moment by watching us put things in Frank's Acura. Her eyes wearied. The late August sun cast shadows on Marie; the house; the driveway; its plush, violet-tinted hydrangeas; Frank; and me. The distribution of light and darkness reminded me that Marie's seventy-ninth birthday honored time, clock time, mnemonic time, body time, and time in the way we talk and listen to one another. The present sharp hour condensed the promises of our tangled family history. Because the day together was about time, it also paid homage to time's offspring, love.

Frank and I stepped into the car and, just like that, Marie was gone.

For all her spunk and animation, Marie was in poorer health than ever on her birthday. The next Tuesday, September 2, I called St. Barnabas Hospital to arrange hospice care, as we had for Nellie. It was too late. Life beat us to Marie. Just as Frank and I were sitting down to dinner of macaroni and salad on Thursday, September 4, Debbie called to say that the Cedar Grove police and emergency squad were at the house. By the time we arrived in the short twilight before evening, Marie was dead. She'd gone for broke and won. No pounding her chest, no paddling, no jamming large needles with drugs, no electric shocks. Being at home under Debbie's watchfulness spared Marie the violent interventions that had grieved her at St. Vincent's. The death certificate listed congestive heart failure as the cause of death. Marie died of having lived. Full of days, she was ready. She lived her death.

On Monday, September 8, 2003, the feast of the Birth of the Virgin Mary, there was the Mass of the Resurrection for Marie. The late summer morning was fair and clement. A small band of friends and relatives attended the simple liturgy at St. Catherine of Siena Church in Cedar Grove, where my sister had been a parishioner for fifty years. As with the service for Nellie, not a personal word was added to the austere biblical readings and prayerful acclamations for the dead. We commended Marie to the absolute freedom she sought. *Salve regina, mater misericorde. Hail Queen, Mother of Mercy and of Love.* Burial was next to Nellie, now a pinch of earth from which we are fashioned, in the ground our mother chose at the Gate of Heaven Cemetery in East Hanover.

The late morning sun was at its ease. Shafts of sunlight flecked the graveside service. Like the bright weather, everything this September day followed the way things had gone nearly eighteen years earlier in January 1986 as a backward nod to Nellie, for the clear horizon unfolding.

9 **Heart's Memory**

Behold, thou desirest truth in the inward being; therefore teach
me wisdom in my secret heart.

—Psalm 51:6

Weary or bitter or bewildered as we may be, God is faithful.
He lets us wander so we will know what it means to come
home.

—Marilynne Robinson, *Home*

The closing of this *vecchia* story tugs at my heart. A once-familiar
female temperament that reached back a millennium across the Atlantic to the flyspeck town of Campochiaro perched in the Abruzzo Mountains was on the way to being forgotten, and there is much about these
ever-plain women I must hold on to.

The Cordileone-Giannone women dramatized an inconspicuous yet
noble chapter in the frequently noisy story of New Jersey Italians. Plug-
ging away in domestic obscurity (dullness to many), they lived out a
saga of uprooting, mother-loss, dementia, solitude, and material concern for others. As aging and mental incapacity drove each woman
into the absolute aloneness of God, her solitude turned daughter after
daughter into mother after mother. Maternal nurture became a patri-
mony. For ten years or so, I helped my sister Marie take care of our
mother, Nellie. Then for seven more years, I looked after Marie. Eventually Marie, the childless daughter, in her mental decline fostered
once more the mother in me, her gay younger brother.

* * *

Fast forward to late 2009. It has been more than two decades now since Nellie died and six years since Marie was buried on September 8, 2003, next to Nellie in the Gate of Heaven Cemetery in East Hanover, New Jersey. The routine business of life goes on. Frank and I still live on Jane Street in the far west corner of Greenwich Village near the Hudson River. Frank is now retired. Prostate cancer is part of his past and, we hope, will remain there. Parkinson's disease will continue to slow him down. That's in the cards. As the brain produces less dopamine, motor neurons lose the ability to transmit movement to the body's extremities. Folding sheets and towels is difficult for him. His handwriting has shrunk to a scrawl. Other faculties are weakening. At this point, Frank has lost the sense of smell, our most basic sense.

Motor disorders are difficult to treat, involving as they do many emotional components. We live from neurologist visit to neurologist visit, in three-month reprieves of concern about an increase in powerful drugs with debilitating side effects, managing fatigue, hoping for the breakthrough in stem cell research. So far Frank, not the disease, has the upper hand. Thanks to a sensitive, patient neurologist and several hours of exercise every morning, he appears in fine shape for a man of sixty-five. He does not have the tremors typical of Parkinson's. Unseen rigidity, nonetheless, stalks him as a constant enemy. Frank rarely tells me about a medical problem or asks for help getting his arm into a jacket. It's up to me wordlessly to lift the sleeve as part of a natural embrace of his shoulder. An onlooker is likely to picture me as the parent dressing a child. It's also my job to tie bows on gifts and unscrew the tops of refrigerated bottles before Frank uses them because Parkinson's makes repeated rotating movements nearly impossible. I aspire to be useful, somehow.

However well Frank is at present, the future sets off my internal alarm if I let it. From time to time I do give way. I dread—well, I'll come out with it—that creeping paralysis will leave Frank with a body he cannot use. As there is no cure for Parkinson's, there is no dispelling this nightmare. Even if such monstrous imprisonment of his spirit does not happen, at length one of us will suffer the loss of the other. Never during meals, but periodically during our walks when we are feeling at ease with the world, we do mull over who will leave this life first. How could we not think about final parting? The subject goes with being lovers. The loneliness of outliving a protective partner of many decades must be exceptionally cruel. At seventy-five I have to prepare myself to lose Frank, as he most likely anticipates being without me. I won't ask Frank not to miss me.

I do have a few posthumous requests. Please, Frank, don't forget that my will is next to the TIAA-CREF retirement documents in the bottom drawer of the bedroom file cabinet. Leave all that stuff to the lawyer. There should be no outstanding bills, but lots of books and papers will turn up around the apartment. Don't fuss. Fordham may want the books. If the library doesn't, there's always the basement laundry room in our building where people look for something to read. By all means, call The Catholic Worker to pick up my clothes and anything else, such as the Mary Frank gouache, that you put up with because I liked it. No need to shred class notes and unfinished essays. Just throw the files away. My innermost thoughts informed what I wrote, but the true record was lived out with you and the old women. Now I cannot imagine that you won't hang on to the ocher-hued Turkish rugs that we accumulated. The carpets are the soul of our home and give so much warm pleasure. Then, just so long as you remember to change the air-conditioner filters for summer and stay abreast with the quirky alternate-side parking regulations, you can ache for me all you need to.

There is no substitute for grieving. Nor is there a timetable or end. I have never understood why lamenting should come to an end. Why expel the dead from our heart? *Closure,* the word used in popular self-help books for grieving, strikes me as suiting financial settlements. Mourning, even if unresolved and wounding, is negative in word only. A sense of deprivation can expand the heart. Grief, the price we pay for love, can unlock the way to a new basis for repose. Finding rest, as you well know, has not been my strong suit. So I'll leave you to your own inner trudging through the dark thickets of loss. That is none of my business.

In this light of remembrance, I see a sign that religion is trying, ever so tactfully, to help a gay person find peace after losing a lover.

In recognition of gay Jews, a new reform prayer book for Rosh Hashanah and Yom Kippur, the *mahzor*, includes for the first time in the prayer for dead relatives a prayer for a deceased "partner." Here, by bringing an ancient ritual of memory in line with contemporary times, is an inkling of love in collective remembrance. It kindles my heart to know that same-sex bonds have found in the synagogue a form of liturgical inclusion. I, for one, take support where I find it. When Frank attends the culminating service of Yom Kippur with our friend Martin and his family, he can remember me with the dignity and spiritual clout of rich Jewish worship.

Keeping death before me has brought unforeseen benefit. Far from being morbid, coming to terms with the losses of Nellie and Marie keeps me alive inside. Their lives proceed in a mnemonic stillness that holds everything in hope. This remembrance, though shaped by failure and reluctance, fosters interior progress. Bereavement prods me along to reconciliation, to put things to rights with final matters. The least-expected effect of being close to death has been the most healing. For all the difficulty of caring for the sick and the harshness of their dying, the final word in the practice is *tenderness*.

Reminiscing about a future without old ties naturally raises threats of emptiness. I am not so much concerned about leaving formal academic work. Don't get me wrong, I will certainly miss the informal intellectual involvement; but research, bright students, and colleagues have always been enabling means to a fuller life of emotional liberty and personal engagement beyond the university. For decades, friends have provided guidance and unfailing support, with Frank at the axis of this loyalty.

After my partnership with Frank, for which Nellie's and Marie's love prepared me, my attending these dying women was the high-water mark of moral learning. With traces of contentment plying across the intimation of their death, the daily rhythm of caregiving belonged to a fresh order of final things. Even though I have made little of these enigmas of life and death, just lingering on them enhanced the days with mystery. Prosaic acts were a religious ceremony. Sponging down their feet felt part of a drama with God.

When I think about Grandma and her female offspring or mention their names, I feel an inner glow. They return like flashes of light in shadows. All are slight figures, always modest, always inhibited, shrinking from brain damage, and yet vividly present. Out of faces scored by the laws of time their liquid eyes beam, eyes that have seen so much misery that death did not surprise them. They had none of the sentimentality that goes with fear of death. Somewhat dimmed by aging, their eyes stayed open to affection. The love of life remained strong in them. By their endurance these women gained their lives and put me on trial.

High tide eventually falls away. The passings of Nellie and Marie lowered the mood in my spirit. It seems like a mistake to be getting old without them. Days feel especially perilous as I approach death with the awareness that I will take the place of the women I attended. Will I receive the gift of steadfastness that kept them vital?

In my anxious turning to the past, my heart's memory gestures toward thanking these *vecchie* who cut lone figures even in the family. To the kindness of these confounding women and the forbidding desert places they enlivened, I owe everything. Repayment was not possible. I feel the need for pardon. I never took care of them as much as I came to love them. Because gifts such as theirs do not go without saying, I want to say that they were given to me for rebuke and comfort. The admonition was to my private will, that will-o'-the-wisp; the reassurance was to my heart.

Every correction must begin somewhere, and the remedial influence came from the bodies of old women. The scourge of illness touched a hidden depth of vitality in them. From that essential deep there stirred a pursuit for the source of life that suggested the sheer size and dynamism of their inner world. Amid final trials an inner pulse strengthened them to ride out wreckage of body and mind toward lasting peace. As the women exposed themselves to the commands of flesh, they cumulatively validated the human body. Their illness held a blessing—in the Old English meaning of *blessing*, that is—to make sacred or holy with blood. Perishable flesh, they showed me, was more than the object of cultural disparagement. I sensed that the body, my body, held more than the fear of erotic adventure that the AIDS crisis magnified into panic.

Through hands-on attention to the physical deterioration marking my mother's protracted dementia and my sister's drawn-out illnesses, a bigger picture came into view. Their bodies organically spooled out a vast, unseen providential design of life and fate. No one else but God could have supplied them with an irreducible inner core; and the center of their soul, which is to say, the total source of life, was in the body. The test for me was not seeing beyond animate existence but responding to the invisible spirit in decaying tissue. The root of and access to salvation had to be in the flesh. Nellie and Marie, however, had remained in possession of their own secrets. Something incorruptible sheltered them. Because human love does not have the power to read the inmost heart of another, I could only imagine what it was like to have one's identity secured in him who created their dying bodies. I wonder how God sees these women.

I am not sure what tells me this, but I knew something was going on. It appeared that for Nellie and Marie to reach the unalloyed wellspring of striving and hope, life had to strip away from them all that was not God. Things seem taken away as quickly as they are given. Because accomplishments were mere decorations, achievements were the first to go. Possessions followed suit. It didn't matter that the house was fully paid for, that there was money in the bank and stocks were paying dividends—these women became poorer. After that, physical power and features of personality went their mutable way. Love, time's offspring, ran out its natural course. The limits of our love perfected our love.

Eventually, it seems, one loses everything, not just conventional social identity but even oneself. Especially oneself. Something replaces the ego. Something unanticipated and more valuable remains. A virginal blankness of utter loss made room for fuller being, for him who made the body. He seems to enter one's life during times of death, sorrow, and self-doubt, when the basis of a person's existence is imperiled or extinguished. At that point, the void opens into a plenum, a desert irradiated by grace.

Just a thought.

* * *

When Nellie and Marie died and no longer had need of me, I had need of them. Each in being delivered from the body of death pointed to the magnetic north of my longing. I roam about seeking a place that is always distant all the while made present by my wanting it. Over the years I have called the objective by many names: *sex, abstinence, university, tenure, health, solitude, justice, rest, trust, church, loss of faith, companionship,* and the old standby, *love.* All provided a genial roof for a while.

Without knowing it, I was looking for home, but the moment I labeled a refuge *home* its safekeeping crumbled. Home—come to think of it—is never stationary. *Home* gathers together breathing spaces and temporary havens on the horizon for me to tiptoe toward or lunge beyond to the peaceful Zion of the heart. Inevitably, I am projecting a home through my wanderer's eye. This dwelling hovers as a site under construction that will take time without end to finish. I can wait.

Home-seeking has been a slog. Promising gratification, self-will throws me off course and right to my demons. A more reliable signpost has been the welfare of others. Nellie's feebleness handed me along. We ate together in her aloneness, she, with her withered fingers taking a grape or a slice of ham, and I absent-minded with little appetite for the food and ceremony. Efforts to tidy up the messiness of daily living with an invalid proved futile. The curtailing of life defined a world of the small and trivial that grew smaller and more consuming. It was harder and harder to be with her. I wanted to flee, but Nellie's hunger and lameness pulled me back. Her body was my ordnance in combating the demon of futility.

I wish I could say that I fully opened my arms to Nellie. I did not. Her clouded brain did to me what I could not have done for her or for myself. She put herself at my bosom. She huddled against me many times, and each nestling jolted me. To my greater surprise, Nellie's frailty didn't crush me. Her devastating illness, instead, was a breaking through. As only a diamond can cut a diamond, only the sharp instrument of her bony frame could have pierced the fear of human attachment occluding my heart. The wound of love exposed a receptiveness to compassionate pain I admire in others but personally could not bear. I had to be wary of living on the edge of a spiritual knife. We rubbed along.

Though Marie, Frank, and I were at Nellie's side, at the end Nellie could count on God alone. Can one put hope in a supreme being one has rejected? I think so. After all, human faithlessness places no limits on divine grace. Besides, it seems to be the scriptural case that we encounter Jesus only unawares. The affecting testimony of the Lord's power came in the air Nellie breathed. No longer needing a little water and a morsel of bread in her final days, Nellie imparted a freedom and corporeal spirit. Absurd though it seemed, her abandonment brought us shelter. We happened upon an oasis of well-being amid fearful desolation.

This home was a point in time. For a split second we lived in the spirit of this time in that place, a center of domestic affection. The instant was ample; it is all. Our true home, I sensed, is in the present moment, if one is sufficiently mindful to yield to its abundance. Yes, I just wish that the submission gave comfort. It did not. I was always conflicted about home.

There's no telling how the body gets the spirit home, or vice versa. Nellie surrendered; Marie did not give an inch and exhibited her claws. The obedience that dementia imposed on Nellie seemed an intentional somatic discipline for Marie. She wouldn't take medicine, hardly ate, and turned her back squarely on my trying to help. In her last years she weighed just over a hundred pounds, iron will and all. Any suggestion to see a physician went in one ear and out the other.

With Marie I was in pitch-dark. I stood by her but not from my deep heart. Her love was there, in her fidelity to Nellie, in her anger, in her reliance on me; but I rarely if ever felt her love. She did not care what I understood about her medical problems or inner life. That struggle was between Marie and the white glass rosary beads tucked under her pillow, where she put self-sorrow, which she believed in as much as she believed in self-esteem. For all I could grasp, Marie may have been renouncing her body to satisfy her soul. She struck me as going into her corner to die. There she seemed to want her life to be a little more difficult than that of most solitaries.

If I could not accompany Marie to death's hideout, I might have stopped trying to drag her back to the futureless state she fixed on leaving. An unfearing sister-child who burns with determination can be hell to live with. Her courage was too sharp and big to fit into my too-tiny heart. When direct contact with life was smack before me, I teetered on the threshold of guilt and sorrow rather than enter the province where true compassion begins. My lean faith had to leave Marie to her personal freedom or to God's favor. I mistook being caregiver with being enforcer, which made life harder for both of us. I am ashamed to remember the harshness of my responses and the pain that severity caused. Trying to help her—or anyone—without compassion cannot be anything but the stubbornness of egotism. My lack of self-awareness got in the way of my feeling her love. That's how it was with my big sister. Again, in drawing as close as I could to Marie, I saw that the limits of human love perfected our love.

Six years after she died, now safe from the raw emotions stirred by Marie's bold choices, I understand that living her own death was her way to get home. And that's how mothering is at life's end, I guess. Like Marie's pressing homeward in chosen obscurity, my mothering was a groping in the dark. There's the nurturing *and* the being nurtured, the holding *and* the letting go *and* the holding all over again. Every turn yields a new catalogue of errors in maternal care. Bearing defeats was part of my plodding home, which waits on the other side of setbacks. Failure for me is the dimension of love by which we judge our individual worth. Humbling as the experience of powerlessness was, each falling short with both women demanded starting anew.

A great deal of the drive of these women was about home: finding a home, keeping the home, protecting the home, and leaving home. They put together a household replete with the usual heartaches and affectionate hopes of family life. Dwelling, nevertheless, eventually meant more than answering a need for shelter and identity. For all the sweat and conviction these women invested in home, they didn't belong there. They knew there was no enduring home, but they never stopped trying to build it.

The material abode with its set street address of decades was undeniably good for immigrants. The house provided a known place in which to breathe the last breath. But this locatedness only partially accounted for what was going on. Some other dwelling in some other country made claims on their efforts. The final years of these homemakers brought to light a radical homesickness in the soul that launched them on a secondary migration. These women were orphans seeking a higher, gracious adoption. The character of that hope was associated with a home timeless in origin and eternal in realization. Finding bodily rest involved ceaseless interior labor.

Although I was not a dying old woman, they made me feel like one of them at their kitchen table and bedside. As we moved back and forth from danger and joy, our relationship seemed inevitable. After perishable flesh shattered the frame of familial life, we had failure and loneliness in common and something to provide one another. There I was, home, the domain of women: Memory was everywhere, and disinclination on my side had been the norm. The aching limits of love distilled home to the capacity to handle human frailty, to forgive another's vices and to watch over those in their distress, when they are hard to take. Strange it is that the domestic source I actively wanted to avoid should be the font I gravitated toward for sustenance.

Home's restricted boundaries took in a spectrum of emotions: There were extremes of bewilderment and restiveness when I was on the ropes; and there was tender cohesion when we were at (or beyond) love. We took care of one another in those moments, keeping the other still in the hints of measureless mercy. Moments of caring became a movement toward union. I may be going too far in describing our coming together. These women, come to think of it, did not have fluid personalities that allowed them easily to merge with others. Emotional display did not gauge their feelings. Nor did words articulate our bonds.

The only proof of our connection came in an ineffable transference. Not explainable because the evidence was like a breeze one couldn't see or hear and could know only by its soft effects. For an instant I felt the unhoped-for grace of being part of a whole. On balance, the time with them could well have been a pretext devised by God to isolate me so that I could see myself in the starkness of humankind's ultimate desire. To those with nothing, God is everything.

By not letting me forget that my ways are before him who sees all, who knows when I stand and when I sit, the *vecchia* story encompasses an ongoing conversion. Conversion? Yet better is *metanoia*, or change of heart, a term from ascetical literature that goes with my anchoritic imagination. The ancient term stresses an interior change involving the orientation of the personality toward God. *Conversion* and its less familiar equivalent *metanoia* are suspect words when reflecting on personal history.

But not always.

I use *metanoia* to soften conversion in its sharpest sense, by which a "reborn" person casts aside past identity and breaks through to a new life and conduct owing nothing to society and everything to God. Far from being that drastic, the shift I feel is a moderating of disposition. The modeling power of institutional Catholicism has given way to the tempering influence of the gospel in its most elemental shape in daily life. The events of Jesus's active life sum up his teaching with radical and realistic simplicity. Faith is an act of heart actualized in human relationships. It is by moving more selflessly toward others that we draw nearer to God. Closeness to Nellie and Marie brought me to feel the possibility of direct contact with something greater than myself. In doing so, they led me to the ground of existence and the essence of church.

Helping these women allowed the creator spirit of life to act in me to set a new direction. I was not asked to do anything myself, but to let something happen to me while respecting my liberty. What came about engendered a process of starting anew, turning around, and persevering. A possibility of inner reform took hold of me. A metanoia.

Because I was raised a Catholic, the change was not from nothing to something. No blinding light made a persecutor into a renegade proselytizer of the faith. Telling people what to believe or not to believe rubs my principles the wrong way. Saving souls has struck me as part of marketplace religion. Nor was the breach from the past wrenching or public. Doctrine and debate were beside the point. My change is more like water getting lost in sand. Martin Luther and John Calvin, having sent a tsunami over the early modern Christian world, would not bat an eye at my slow modern drift; but they might recognize in my reform their legacy of measuring personal belief and good conscience against the gospel, the basis of genuine reformation.

I should add that I did not grow up in a household that knew the Bible; nor was scripture part of my formal education. The Hebrew and Greek texts came to me much later in response to curiosity about the struggles of a believing community epitomized in the transforming event called Jesus. When these testaments finally reached me, their stories turned bedtime blessing, catechetical apologetics, and rigid belief system into mystery. Shadows and experience to the contrary complicated childhood formulas about meaning and misery. Then much later, the old women put flesh on my questions about the giver of life and what might lie beyond the grave before me. Simply put, a new mood stirred a hidden compunction and suffused how I thought about what mattered.

The subdued reform that I am describing expressed itself in the tenor of responding to people. I moved away from the usual inert debate and dry-as-dust politics about religion toward the call of love. Nellie's word was silent. By contrast, Marie's sharp voice in various ways and situations made that summons poignantly clear. Her desperation, reproach, and bewilderment were appeals for freedom. Such freedom is fulfilled by a readiness to obey not the law but the calling.

The directive I answered was to another man and to the uncomely flesh of dying women, paired aspects of one call. My limited capacity for love required accepting their love to complete it. The best way I can explain such responses was an effort to be useful. Practical acts trained my heart. Learning to love another man and old women and being torn from them replaced all systems of belief and knowledge with increasing mystery and uncertainty. Bottomless mystery deepened my insecurity and bedeviling unbelief.

Spiritual search turns for some people on what happens to their person or to their possessions or to the imbalance of justice in the public sphere; for others, faith is what comes to pass in their emotions and human connections. So it was in my experience with the women in my family. Warming to the task of aloneness, they made friends with diminishing life. From the cradle they were on familiar terms with death many years before they came to die. At long last, they gave up the struggles of the complicated decades of hopes, false and genuine, that were ending. By befriending death, they were no longer victims. Intriguingly, their souls prospered as their bodies weakened.

Dying was an act of communicating anew. These women developed the strength to be grateful. Each no longer was afraid to show love as loving. That's gutsy. Love, as a quality of being and not just a passion, was a discovery about life for me, a disclosure of love as a believing force. Love, in acknowledging dependence, puts its trust in the supernatural. Home is part of the soul. Let come what may, they were at home on their long, uncharted way home.

Without ever talking about, or in Nellie's case without acknowledging God, these women conveyed a humble receptivity to his unbidden help. With my mother, God used her rejection of him to win over acknowledgement in me. He acted immediately with what he had, and in mystifying silence. Although Nellie's and Marie's fleshly erosions told the familiar human story of mortality, a felt inner force animating their personalities made sickness and dying about much more than extinction. There were stirrings of the principle of life, the Logos, the essential truth of Christianity that could rouse anyone anytime. Fire burns under ashes.

These women left no library by which biographers could probe the inner workings that guided them. They did leave a house, but that structure, as things go, is now in other hands. Memory is the sole hook. Those who gained most from them were those who saw and heard them and, best of all, had physical contact with the quality of their loyalty to others. Personal transmission surpassed dogma in awakening faith. Their disabled and knowing bodies intimated the spirit and work of God, which the Syriac tradition envisaged, and I imagined, as feminine.

Mothering Nellie and Marie while loving Frank has made Christianity far more than a preset scheme, put together for all time, of truths that must be agreed to and maintained factually. This master plan may be true for some, but I have had to look elsewhere for trust. I sought help in the boundaries of our being as we worked out our lives through trying times and in harsh, perilous places. Gauging those limits was the condition of seeking faith. In the wake of human experience, faith, which is to say our humanness, comes into being. These moments of touching the edge of truth are religion. They bring us into contact with our essential self that is buried beneath resentment and fear. This true self seeks and must come out of hiding. Gay or straight, so long as we remain hidden from ourselves, the true God remains hidden from us. Nellie and Marie taught me that personal integrity before God, without masks and false hopes, is the intrinsic nature of faith.

In this inward negotiation, the *vecchia* spirit is my mistress and balances my life in its grip. Feeling deserted in time of trouble perhaps holds the *vecchia*'s sturdiest wisdom about kinship with the divine, which comes to us in secret. I would like to walk in the counsel of Grandma, Nellie, and Marie down the hidden ways to the veiled God, but they left me at the crossroad where they left one another. At Nellie's deathbed Marie called out, "What do I do now?"

I have often thought of Marie's outburst. Her vehemence seemed uncalled for until I heard it resonate with an episode in John's gospel. At the end of his public life, Jesus announces that he is leaving to be with the Father. With suffering and brutal execution lying ahead, the disciples' hearts are troubled. Jesus's response and departure provide a coda to his teaching: "I have yet many things to say to you, but you cannot bear them now" (John 16:12).

Jesus leaves his followers in dire suspense. They have to wonder what those "many things" are. Jesus shies away from any final truth about his friends' relation to the world. "When the Spirit of truth comes, he will guide you into all the truth" (John 16:13). As if to avoid a rigid concept of the Father that could lead to presumption, Jesus leaves matters in the balance of human quest and individual liberty.

Jesus's destabilizing words are at once a prayer and an introduction to the mystery at the foundation of the good news. Bafflement about what Jesus had to say reaches full depth when his empty tomb is discovered by—of all observers—women, who in Jewish law are unreliable witnesses. The account of the risen life ends with those women present at the sepulchre dumbstruck, "for they were afraid" (Mark 16:8). The prince of peace who worked wonders turns out to be a master of perplexity with no end of corners and dark clouds in which to abscond. To take Jesus to heart is to live with absence, open questions, and dissent. Risk and uncertainty lie at the battered heart of Christianity. Because I can neither resolve the contradictions within me nor rise above them, I must live with them. And wait and listen for the voice of silence.

I find myself back in Palestine with those men hearing Jesus's parting words and with those women at the first Easter. Jesus made a point of leaving followers just at the beginning of seeking. Given the doubt and disappearance that beset faith, the anguish of acceptance must be a mere preliminary to the perseverance needed to navigate the obscure tunnel ahead. Mistrustful about "the things that are to come" (John 16:13), I am left with personal freedom cloaked in self-interest.

God will have to take me as I am and evermore shall be. For him who dined with sinners, tax collectors, and the uncircumcised who did not follow Mosaic law, that should be no obstacle. While waiting for rescue from old life, I thread my tangled way down Bleecker Street to settle in a back pew at St. Joseph's 5:30 weekday liturgy hopeful for new. The table is set. Several undergraduates toting swollen backpacks hasten to join the ever-punctual elderly. To the left, the Puerto Rican woman missing her left eye discreetly nods hello. The presider clears his throat. I await the asking the Lord be with us.

Acknowledgments

My gratitude goes, first and foremost, to Fordham University. Only its welcome and backing for more than four decades could have made it possible for me to develop as a teacher and a writer. I am mindful also of a debt to my students. Year after year, their enthusiasm and curiosity challenged and strengthened my fascination with the bearing of religion on literature. These reflections have benefited from many friends and colleagues who encouraged me when writing, and who heartened me when I couldn't write. Because their varied help and kindness go beyond the formal limits of an acknowledgment, I settle for naming them without individual emphasis. My thanks to Emma Cordileone, Paul Elie, Mary Erler, Maria Farland, Wendy Gimbel, Susan Greenfield, Elizabeth Ann Johnson, Eve Keller, Mark Massa, A. G. Mojtabai, Angela Alaimo O'Donnell, Joyce Rowe, Phil Sicker, Kathy Stanzione, Joe Wholey, Midge Wholey, T. P. Winch, and Diane Zahler. Special thanks go to Fred Nachbaur, director of Fordham University Press, for his support in shaping the book, and to Eric Newman, managing editor of the Press. Last of all, my partner, Frank, and long-time friend Joe Sendry have schooled me in the power of Augustine's observation that a friend is "one with whom one may dare to share the counsels of one's heart."

New York
July 2011